Fishing New Jersey

A Guide for Freshwater Anglers

OLIVER SHAPIRO

BURFORD BOOKS

Printed in the United States of America.

10 9 8 7 6 5 4 3 2 1

Library of Congress Cataloging-in-Publication Data
Shapiro, Oliver.
    Fishing New Jersey : a guide for freshwater anglers /
by Oliver Shapiro.
        p.   cm.
    Includes index.
    ISBN-13: 978-1-58080-140-9
    ISBN-10: 1-58080-140-4
    1. Fishing—New Jersey—Guidebooks.   2. New Jersey—
Guidebooks. I. Title.

SH525.S53   2006
799.1'109749—dc22

                                        2006025619

Contents

MAPS

Northern New Jersey
(Locations approximate)

1 Barbours Pond
2 Bear Swamp Brook
3 Bear Swamp Lake
4 Big Flat Brook
5 Black River
6 Branch Brook Park Pond
7 Budd Lake
8 Canistear Reservoir
9 Clinton Reservoir
10 Cranberry Lake
11 Deer Park Pond
12 Delaware River
   (Northern sections)
13 Echo Lake
14 Furnace Lake
15 Green Turtle Pond
16 Greenwood Lake
17 Grover Cleveland
   Park Pond
18 Hainesville Pond
19 Jefferson Lake
20 Lake Aeroflex
21 Lake Ames
22 Lake Hopatcong

23 Lake Musconetcong
24 Lincoln Park Lake
25 Merrill Creek Reservoir
26 Monksville Reservoir
27 Mount Hope Pond
28 Mountain Lake
29 Musconetcong River
30 Oak Ridge Reservoir
31 Passaic River
32 Pequest River
33 Ramapo Lake
34 Ramapo River
35 Rockaway River
36 Ryker Lake
37 Saddle River
38 Scarlet Oak Pond
39 Swartswood Lake
40 Van Campens Brook
41 Verona Park Lake
42 Wanaque River
43 West Hudson County
   Park Pond
44 White Lake
45 Woodcliff Lake

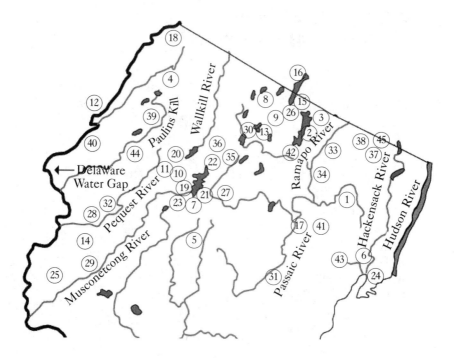

Delaware
Water Gap

Central New Jersey
(Locations approximate)

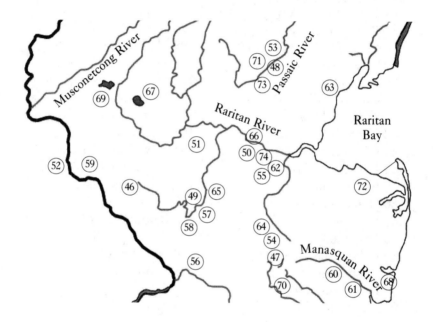

Southern New Jersey
(Locations approximate)

75 Alcyon Lake
76 Bargaintown Pond
77 Birch Grove Park Ponds
78 Blackwood Lake
79 Cape May County Park
80 Clarks Pond
81 Colliers Mills and
  Turn Mill Ponds
82 Cooper River Waters
83 Dennisville Lake
84 East Creek Pond
85 Elmer Lake
86 Hammonton Lake
87 Harrisonville Lake
88 Iona Lake
89 Lake Carasaljo and
  Lake Manetta
90 Lake Nummy
91 Lake Shenandoah
92 Laurel Acres Park Pond
93 Laurel Lake
94 Lenape Lake
95 Makepeace Lake

96 Malaga Lake
97 Maple Lake
98 Maskells Mill Pond
99 Maurice River and
  Menantico Creek
100 Menantico Sand Ponds
101 Metedeconk River
102 Mirror Lake
103 Mullica River
104 New Brooklyn Lake
105 Parvin Lake
106 Pemberton Lake
107 Prospertown Lake
108 Rainbow Lake
109 Rancocas Creek
110 Strawbridge Lake
111 Sunset Lake
112 Sylvan Lakes
113 Toms River
114 Union Lake
115 Willow Grove Lake
116 Wilson Lake

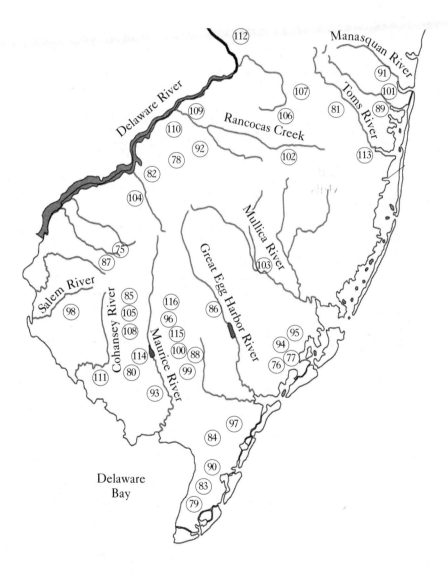

Manasquan River

Delaware River

112

107

91

101

Toms River

106

81

89

109

Rancocas Creek

110

102

113

92

78

82

104

Mullica River

75

103

87

Salem River

Great Egg Harbor River

85

116

86

98

105

96

108

115

95

Cohansey River

114

100

88

94

99

Maurice River

76

77

111

80

93

97

Delaware
Bay

84

90

83

79

ACKNOWLEDGMENTS

THE FIRST AND most important person I need to thank is my wife, Debby. She is at the same time my severest critic and most enthusiastic supporter. She has always provided help whenever it was needed, encouragement when it was desired, and a kick in the pants when it was least wanted but most necessary. And despite her continued wonderment at how a grown man could be so obsessed with the pursuit of some cold-blooded and usually slimy creatures, Debby still has no problems with me going on these outings and even listens to my fish stories with interest.

There's also my father, who despite limited interest in angling nevertheless has supported my needs and interests throughout my life, and more importantly expended so much time and effort in his never-ending efforts to raise his two sons properly. Pop, I hope that as the world observes Alex and me, it becomes clear that your efforts have been validated. Personally, I can't imagine anybody doing a better job.

I must also thank my mother, may she rest in peace. Mom was a traditional stay-at-home mother for the vast majority of my formative years. She seemed a little taken aback when I first started showing a propensity for writing about outdoor experiences, but she took a shine to it after a while, and soon became a full member of my small but dedicated cheering section. She was more pleased, I think, than anybody when I sold my first fishing article to the *Dateline Journal* of Passaic County, and she watched my writing career accelerate with what I believe to be genuine pride. I miss you, Mom.

My three sons, Zack, Ozzie, and Max, are the best. Although none of them has completely gone over the edge in fishing, each has become a fair angler in his own way. Zack seems to gravitate toward surf angling, Ozzie enjoys fly fishing for trout, and Max likes fishing for bass in ponds. Of all my angling companions, these three are hands-down the greatest.

There's another special debt that I need to pay, and that is to Milt Rosko, one of the greatest saltwater fishing anglers and writers in America. When Peter Burford of Burford Books asked Milt—who had already authored multiple books for Peter's company—whom he thought might be qualified and interested in writing a book such as this one, to my great surprise Milt mentioned my name. Milt, if a few anglers increase their enjoyment of New Jersey's freshwater angling as a result of these efforts, then you'll have done good.

And of course there's Peter Burford. Of the many editors I've worked with over the years, Peter shows unusual patience and tolerance. His skills in envisioning a book and bringing it through to completion are unmatched, and he is one of the easiest people to work with that you could hope to meet. Thanks for everything, Peter.

As far as information for this book goes, there are innumerable people to thank; it will be impossible to list them all here. Some have provided very specific details about this or that, while others have contributed to my general knowledge of one or more sections in the very broad subject known as freshwater fishing, especially in New Jersey. (I'm sure that I will omit a few crucial names, and to those whom I may miss, I hope you will accept my apology, and special thanks for your past help.) Some of these people include the following.

Current and former employees of the New Jersey Division of Fish and Wildlife: Lisa Barno, Dave Chanda, Pat Hamilton, Al Ivany, Bob McDowell, Marty McHugh, Bob Olson, Bob Papson, Jim Sciascia, Bob Soldwedel, and Paul Tarlowe.

Various members and organizations within New Jersey's bass-fishing community: the New Jersey Bass Federation, the South Jersey Hawg Hunters Bass Club, Nick Benigno, Rick Faulkner, Tony Going, and Paul Renaldo. The professional anglers in this group, particularly Pete Gluszek and Mike Iaconelli, are worthy of special mention. Both these guys are unbelievable anglers, and also just great folks to work and fish with. Their knowledge seems to be bottomless, and they have always been happy to share as much of it as I could absorb.

Members and organizations representing the Garden State's trout-angling community, including the different Trout Unlimited chapters, Dan Drozdowski, Rick Ege, and Gerard Richelo.

Those who represent the muskellunge's interests in its new home waters. The New Jersey chapter of Muskies, Inc., and Bruce Ruppel have always been there when I needed them.

The Lake Hopatcong Knee Deep Club, which has always been available for help, information, and more. Special thanks go to Tim Clancy, Lou Marcucci, and Jim Salerno.

The incredible knowledge possessed in aggregate by New Jersey's sporting goods stores. In a great many critical ways, these folks are the backbone of fishing and other outdoor pursuits in New Jersey—or anywhere else, for that matter. Some of those that have been of inestimable help to me (and a few of these have, unfortunately, been consigned to oblivion) are Adventure Sports, Assunpink Bait and Tackle, Bait and Boat, Blackwater Sports Center, Britts Bait and Tackle, Bruno's Bait and Tackle, Clinton Outfitters, County Line Sport Shop, Degnaro's, Delaware River Outfitters, Dow's Boat Rental, Fairfield Tackle Store, Fly Fishing Plus, The Fly Fishing Shop, Frank's Tackle, Greenwood Lakes Sports Center, Hainesville Sporting Goods, Lebanon Bait and Sports Shop, Maurice River Sports Center, Monksville Bait and Tackle, Parsippany Bait Sport and Tackle, Ramsey's Outdoor Stores, S&B Sportsmen Shop, Shannon's Fly and Tackle Shop, Simon-Peter Sport Company, Sportsmen's Center, Streams of Dreams, and Tom's Tackle Shop.

There are a good number of great fishing guides serving anglers' needs in New Jersey, and knowing many of them has been a great boon to me. These include John Brylinski of Muskie Daze, Ben Iradi, Eugene Niederlander of Fish Assured, Ed Sekula, Ray "Peewee" Serfass, and Cliff Tinsman.

Finally, to all those I have fished with over the years, be it once, a few times, or regularly: I have learned something from all of you, and I thank you.

INTRODUCTION:
A Study in Impossible Juxtapositions

AS THE MOST densely populated state in America, with way more than our fair share of urban centers, developments, and just plain "civilization," New Jersey's fishing opportunities in many ways just keep getting better. More and more lands are purchased by the state Department of Environmental Protection, affording greater access to fishing destinations by more people, even while the developers continue their hungry gobbling of available lands for houses, condos, and the like.

An aggressive Division of Fish and Wildlife provides more and more fisheries in more and more locations, many of them established as self-sustaining populations in enhanced ecological systems. A number of the bodies of water, large and small alike, have been "adopted" by local fishing clubs, which keep an eye on the health and welfare of their chosen waters.

Consider that, before modern wildlife and fisheries management techniques came along, there were darn few fish in New Jersey that anybody would have considered gamefish. The small list included pickerel, sunfish, perch, and some brook trout (called "native trout" back in those days) in some rivers and streams. By the mid-1800s, efforts to bring in other species like largemouth and smallmouth bass started making some changes, and the years since then have brought on a multitude of other varieties—northern pike, rainbow and brown trout, walleye, channel catfish, carp, muskellunge, lake trout, and more.

As this book was in production, in May 2006, the New Jersey Division of Fish and Wildlife stocked some landlocked salmon—a variety of Atlantic salmon—into Aeroflex and Wawayanda Lakes. This bids fair to be a very exciting new fishery; for more information, contact the division (see this book's afterword for contact information).

The bottom line is that the Garden State's waterways are now filled with a plentiful and variegated spectrum of gamefish.

The opportunities can be surprisingly rewarding. I recall, not too many years ago, having the chance to fish Lake Mohawk in Sparta (surrounded by a private community) for bass in late spring, and then a week later traveling to Florida to try my hand at fabled Lake Okeechobee for largemouths. The comparison between the two was reminiscent of David and Goliath, as the action, quantity, and quality of fish was immeasurably higher at the Lake Sparta excursion than Okeechobee.

And where else along the eastern seaboard will you find the incredible opportunities for muskellunge angling that you find in New Jersey? The fishery is so healthy and vibrant that I know of at least one fishing guide who specializes in trips to Greenwood Lake and elsewhere for muskies, where the "fish of 10,000 casts" is caught

Who says sunnies are just for kids? These willing little fighters can put a smile on almost anybody's face.

with far greater frequency than its nickname would have you believe. The New Jersey chapter of Muskies, Inc.—that venerable conservation group dedicated to the continued and improved angling opportunities for this fantastic fish—is the easternmost in the nation.

There are plenty of other examples that illustrate this, and they cover walleye, northern pike, striped bass and hybrids thereof . . . the list is indeed a long one. Suffice it to say that anybody who may denigrate the angling opportunities in New Jersey really has a lot to learn.

• • •

There are over 120 specific bodies of water, all with public access, throughout the Garden State that are discussed in this book. This may seem like a lot, but there are many, many more that aren't included here. Waters were selected based on a number of factors, including my personal familiarity with the location, its ease of access to the public, the quality of the fishing opportunities to be had there, and the importance of that specific location (for whatever reason) to an angler.

Having said that, I must stress that there are a great many places where you can find angling that is as good as, or perhaps even better than, some of the locations discussed here. Why weren't they included? Decisions had to be made, and inclusion of a few other locations could easily have meant bumping some that did make the cut. If you have heard of Lake X, or happen to have it as a pet fishing location, and it isn't found within these pages, that should not be construed at all to mean that I don't consider it a worthwhile fishery. Even as I sit typing these words, I can recall some of the places that I considered including here . . . that never made it to the final draft.

This, in turn, brings up another important point. It's very rewarding indeed to learn of a specific fishery, read about it, go there, and catch plenty of quality fish—in fact, if I could be assured of this happening every time I went fishing, my life would have taken on a definite dreamlike quality. But the rewards of such a scenario pale significantly next to the pleasure of finding and exploring a waterway on your own, unlocking its secrets, and having plenty of great pictures to share with your pals. As Mark Rosewater (who works for a subsidiary of Hasbro Toys) remarked recently, "Working for a victory is a far greater pleasure than having one handed to you." Although I wouldn't say that reading about a spot, incorporating the information learned, and catching fish is exactly having a victory handed to you, I think you see my point.

To that end, I encourage you to spend some time exploring. There are innumerable bodies of water on county maps that aren't named, and by the same token there are lots of watery places holding plenty of great fishing opportunities that you can't even spot on those maps. Many are open to public access, and may or may not be well known to the local fishing fraternity. Even if they're on private lands, it is by no means uncommon for a landowner to grant you permission to fish the water as long as you don't abuse the privilege by making a mess, causing a disturbance, or otherwise being an ungrateful guest. Remember, the worst that can happen is that a landowner will simply say no.

Anytime you're traveling about in your vehicle, take note of your surroundings. Are you on, or did you just pass, a road that's called something like Brookside Drive? How do you think it got its name? Or if it's early in the morning and you're suddenly hit by a bright glare coming through a stand of trees on one side of the road, it could be that there's a pond in there of which you were unaware. What is perhaps my favorite bass pond in New Jersey is located just out of sight along a nearly rural roadway in the northwestern part of the state; it has an amazing largemouth population, it's as peaceful and beautiful as you can get on a summer evening, and very few people ever seem to fish it. I've never even learned if it has a name or not; my sons and I refer to it as "Noname Pond." (No, I won't tell you where it is, and don't bother to ask.)

Talk to other anglers, the clerks in the sports shops, the cashier at the local 7-Eleven when you buy your coffee or soda. You never can tell when you might get that nugget of information that can lead to a whole new world of fishing.

• • •

Throughout this volume there will be references to various baits, tackle, riggings, or techniques that are recommended for a certain place or situation. You'd be wise to consider these as starting points only. There are relatively few times that only a single bait or presentation will catch fish, and all anglers develop their own style and strengths as they go along. Although the methods I'll discuss have been shown to be effective, they may not work as well under the exact set of circumstances in which you find yourself, and your style of fishing may indicate that a different approach could work better. Never be afraid to try something different, especially if it makes sense to you.

The same is true of specific spots. I've tried to mention a number of general or specific places at many of the destinations where the fishing has been proven, but never be afraid to trust your own judgment. In his classic book *Trout*, Ray Bergman wrote the following:

> Most of us have so little time, . . . we think we must fish the best-looking spots where everyone else fishes because they must be good or no one else would fish them. This is false reasoning, because we are relying on precedents established by easy fishing and in most cases by anglers who have followed the established rules rather than the dictates of their own minds. It would pay larger dividends if we spent more time at thinking and observing than at fishing. Remember that locating fish is more than half the battle. When

you know exactly where they are, then you can intelligently fish for them. Otherwise you are simply trusting to luck.

And the more you fish and the more you find what seems to work and what doesn't, the more your powers of judgment will prove increasingly reliable.

Good luck, and good fishing!

A Note on Regulations

Any regulations I discuss in this book are subject to change; however, those I mention throughout are those that have been in force for some time and are, in my estimate, unlikely to change for the foreseeable future.

1

FISH SPECIES

Largemouth Bass (*Micropterus salmoides*)

Largemouth bass are well distributed throughout New Jersey in numerous lakes, reservoirs, streams, and rivers. Anglers who seek them can zoom about in a high-powered bass boat at Lake Hopatcong or Greenwood Lake, or gently probe a quiet stream like the Passaic River.

Those who target this worthy bandit begin their serious quests in early to midspring. You may legally cast for and catch them all year, but between April 15 and June 15, all bass caught must be immediately released. During the remaining 10 months, the daily limit is five (total largemouth and/or smallmouth), each of which must be at least 12 inches.

The largemouth bass is one of America's favorite gamefish, and its following in New Jersey is no less enthusiastic, with plenty of bass-angling clubs (over 50 of them just in the New Jersey Bass Federation) going strong. It has all the characteristics of a good gamefish: It's prevalent in most fresh waters. It presents enough of a challenge to catch so that it never becomes boring, yet at the same time can be enticed to take a bait under most conditions if the diligent angler hits on the right pattern. It fights well when hooked, providing good strong runs and occasional airborne leaps. And it can grow to decent size; the state record is just shy of 11 pounds, and 5-, 6-, and 7-pounders are caught with regularity.

Also known as mossback, bucketmouth, or bigmouth, this fish is easily identified by its distinctively football-like shape, its prominent single dark lateral stripe, and the large mouth. (You can readily distinguish it from its relative the smallmouth bass by observing how far back the mouth extends along the head—if this goes past the eye, it's a largemouth.) The coloring can vary, depending on its environment, but the fish is generally some shade of greenish olive on the back and sides, with a white or yellowish belly.

The vast majority of largemouth bass are caught during open-water seasons, but they do occasionally come up through the ice. The angler shown here hooked this one while targeting northern pike at Budd Lake.

In its behavior, the largemouth is highly structure-oriented. It will hang out in weeds, near rocks, close to bottom, or in other places where it can relate to objects or cover. Forage consists of practically anything it can put in its sizable maw. Smaller, younger individuals will subsist on insects and tiny baitfish; as they increase in size, the menu begins to include larger fish, crayfish, small amphibians, small or immature birds (such as ducklings), and small rodents.

In spring, they begin to move toward shallow areas to prepare for spawning, typically over gravelly bottoms where nests can be easily made. After laying their eggs, the females retreat to deeper waters, and males—after fertilizing the eggs—stay around the nest to guard the eggs until hatching. During this time, they do not feed but will aggressively attack any intruding creatures or objects. Soon after the eggs hatch, the males quit the nest.

By then it's late spring or so, and both males and females will embark on their classic hot-weather daily cycle: staying in deeper waters during the day, moving into shallower waters to feed toward the end of the day, and then returning to deep waters after the first couple of hours of daylight.

With the onset of autumn, largemouths typically feed more aggressively for a few weeks; as the days shorten and water temperatures decrease, they spend more and more time in deeper waters. By the time winter hits, they reach a near-dormant state at the bottom of their home water. I say *near*-dormant because they still exhibit some feeding behavior, as evidenced by the occasional largemouth caught by ice fishermen.

As an aside, it's worth noting that although this is the generally accepted pattern of largemouth behavior, there are plenty of times they seem to be unaware of the rules. It's worth keeping a keen eye on conditions and being prepared to approach the fish as warranted.

Preferred baits include crankbaits, spinnerbaits, various topwater plugs and poppers, soft plastic imitations (worms and soft jerkbaits), jigs, and live offerings like nightcrawlers, shiners, and herring.

Smallmouth Bass (*Micropterus dolomieui*)

No less a fishing legend than Bill Dance has declared that if he were restricted to only one species of North American gamefish, it would be the smallmouth bass. And with good reason. Pound for pound, these feisty battlers give some of the greatest fights to be found in our waters. Similar in overall appearance to the largemouth, they typically have a somewhat slimmer look, especially among river dwellers. Coloring along the back and sides can be browner or somewhat coppery (hence the nickname *bronzeback*), and the mouth extends back such that its rearmost tip is aligned with the eye. There are often dark vertical bars along the side, and three dark bars radiating from the eye.

Creel and size limits were adjusted over a decade ago to conform to those governing largemouth bass; apparently the state Division of Fish and Wildlife believed that too many people had difficulty distinguishing the two species.

They can be found in many river and streams, as well as in larger lakes and impoundments with sufficiently deep and/or cool water. The biggest specimens are in still waters, but river dwellers usually have greater strength and fighting stamina. In rivers, they can found in cooler and faster stretches than those frequented by largemouths, and in lakes and reservoirs they may be found in areas inhabited by largemouths, although they often show a preference for boulders and rock piles.

Unlike largemouths, smallmouths tend to stay in a given area most of the time and don't show as much seasonal or daily wandering, with the exceptions of seeking deeper waters in winter and suitable spawning areas in spring. As soon as known (or even likely) habitat has been identified, you can be reasonably confident that those waters will continue to harbor fish.

Smallmouth feeding preferences include crayfish, baitfish, insects, and amphibians. Bait selections are similar to those for largemouths, but usually in diminished sizes.

Trout (*Salmo* and *Salvelinus* spp.)
Brown, brook, and rainbow trout abound in many New Jersey streams and lakes, and lake trout prowl a couple of the deeper impoundments. Although a large number are intended as put-and-take fish, many of these hold over far beyond the spring trout activity, resulting in a year-round fishery.

Besides the abundant river and lake fisheries, there are also numerous small flows designated Wild Trout Streams, in which no trout are stocked. These are managed to maximize natural trout reproduction, and are known for the colorful and feisty fish they produce amid a nearly pristine wilderness setting. Check for special regulations concerning these waters.

Peaking during the spring and autumn months, trout fishing in New Jersey takes a number of forms—from the classic image of the lone wader-clad fly fisherman in the riffles of a fast-moving river, to the father and son standing next to their worm container on the shores of a small lake, to the boat fisherman deep-trolling the depths of a large impoundment seeking double-digit-pound brown or lake trout specimens.

Trout season begins the second weekend in April, and for many anglers this signals the unofficial beginning of fishing season in general. The truth of the matter is, however, that it's possible to fish for trout year-round in New Jersey, although during the few weeks prior to the April opening such fishing is restricted to a very select few waters, catch-and-release only. In general, the daily limit is six trout from the April opener through the end of May, and four fish at other times that catch-and-keep angling is available. Each fish must be at least 7 inches. But there are numerous exceptions depending on time and place, and I urge you to consult the most recent issue of the *New Jersey Fish and Wildlife Digest* (freshwater fishing issue) available. Too, lake trout have their own regulations: Fishing is open all year except for mid-September through November, and the daily limit is either one or two fish, depending on location, each of which must be at least 15 or 20 inches—again, depending on location.

Inexperienced anglers sometimes have difficulty distinguishing the three stream varieties (brown, brook, and rainbow trout), but a few simple rules can help keep things straight. First, look for a single pink lateral stripe along each side. If it's there, you have a rainbow trout. If not, look at the pectoral fins and the markings along the fish's back. If the fins have a white margin on the leading edges, and the back has light, worm-shaped markings, you have a brook trout. If none of the above applies, it's a brown, and this is confirmed by brown or yellow sides populated with black—and a few orange or red—spots, usually with light halos. Lake trout are a breed apart, and are easily distinguished from the others by their deeply forked tails.

Common wisdom has it that brook trout are the easiest to catch, browns the wariest, and rainbows in between, with a more pronounced tendency to jump when hooked. But fishing is fishing, and I've had days when I couldn't buy a bite from brookies while the browns fell all over themselves in their rush to get hooked.

Recently, the Division of Fish and Wildlife has established a sea-run brown trout program in the Manasquan River (see chapter 9). Fish ranging from the 7- to 8-pound range on up to 13 pounds have been caught.

Popular trout waters tend to be crowded during the first six weeks of the season, and especially the first week. But once June settles in, much of the crowd has dispersed, making for easier access and more casting room. Many of the put-and-take trout are long gone, of course, but the fishing remains good in many waters until well into autumn.

River and stream trout are reasonably predictable in where they can be found. Good locations include down- or upstream from midcurrent rocks and boulders, hiding beneath undercut banks, lurking in weed beds, at the head or tail of deeper pools, and within riffles that have at least nominal depth. Selecting which of these is best at a given moment depends on the season, time of day, and existing weather conditions.

One trick worth trying is to reach into the water and pick up a fist-sized rock from the bottom. Look at its underside for any insect larval forms that may have been hiding there. This will tell you two things. First, the presence of such critters is evidence of an ecosystem likely to support trout, increasing the likelihood that they're present. Second, identifying the larval varieties can help you decide which baits—real or imitation—are more likely to produce.

Although sometimes quite selective, trout will take a huge variety of offerings. Just a few of the popular formulas in New Jersey include fly patterns (dry flies, nymphs, and streamers), lures (small crankbaits, spinners, and spoons), and natural baits (earthworms, fathead minnows, mealworms, salmon eggs, hellgrammites, and PowerBaits).

Landlocked Salmon (*Salmo salar*)

This impressive fish was a late addition to this volume, as the New Jersey Division of Fish and Wildlife announced in spring 2006 new stockings of what until now has been, to many of the state's veteran anglers, only a fond memory. The landlocked salmon is one of the primary varieties of Atlantic salmon, and in areas that don't allow access to the sea, individuals can get as big as 22 pounds (the world record, caught in Maine in 1907). They're unlikely to become that massive hereabouts, however; the existing state-record fish, caught in 1951 from what is now Aeroflex Lake, weighed 8 pounds.

They can be identified by their general troutlike appearance, and of the three stream trout in New Jersey, landlocks most closely resemble brown trout. They may be differentiated from the latter by a slightly more deeply forked tail; also, the spots dotting their sides do not have the smoothly circular shape typical of brown trout.

Chain Pickerel (*Esox niger*)

This toothy gamefish has provided intense enjoyment for countless generations of anglers both young and old, and quite frankly New Jersey is one of the very best states for this game warrior. Specimens are typically encountered in the 1- to 3-pound range, and many individuals exceeding 5 pounds are wrested from our waters each year. It is easily identified by its long, pikelike body and the unmistakable chainlike markings on each side.

The pickerel can be found in most waters that boast a bass population, and many that don't—thanks in large part to its superior tolerance to acidic conditions, accounting for its prevalence in central and southern New Jersey waters including those in the Pine Barrens. It remains more active than many other varieties during the colder months and has no closed season, making it a true year-round fishery. In summertime, it often accounts for nonstop action, and during winter it's probably pulled through the ice more than any other large predator fish.

Habitat preferences are somewhat similar to those for largemouth bass, but think weeds first. Chances are, if you're not catching pickerel from the weed beds of whatever water you're fishing, then either the pickerel population is poor there, or you're doing something wrong.

In some waters—notably slower backwaters and tributaries of rivers, and backwater sections of ponds and lakes—you might encounter the redfin or grass pickerel, the smaller cousin of the chain. On very light tackle, they can be fun to catch, but their diminutive size (the world record is less than 2 pounds) tends to keep them under most fishermen's radar.

The cooperative pickerel attacks a large variety of natural and artificial baits. The daily limit in most waters (check for exceptions) is five per day, with no minimum size restriction (except in a few selected lakes, where the minimum is 15 inches).

Pike and Muskellunge
(*Esox lucius* and *E. masquinongy*)

These two larger members of the pickerel family are well represented in our state. The northern pike has been successfully stocked in some northern New Jersey bodies of water and may be sought year-round, although most are taken during cooler months, and often through the ice. Places like Budd

Lake, Farrington Lake, Spruce Run Reservoir, and Deal Lake have been producing specimens up to the state record of 30 pounds. Some northern river systems like the Passaic and Pompton Rivers, have these gamefish in serious numbers as well.

Since the mid-1980s, New Jersey has been developing a muskellunge fishery that can make your eyes pop. Full-strain specimens are available in the Delaware River and some of the northern lakes, and specimens of 20, 30, and even 40 pounds are now being caught (the state record of nearly 43 pounds was caught in Monksville Reservoir in January 1997 by an ice fisherman). This notorious "fish of 10,000 casts" has created quite a following in its time here in New Jersey, and dedicated anglers are finding that proper attention to the correct locations and techniques can pay very big dividends.

Tiger muskies, the sterile hybrid of pike and muskellunge, have also been planted in widespread stockings throughout the state. This variety is characterized by its large size (although not as big as full-strain muskies), tolerance to a fair range of water qualities, and a greater willingness to strike than its larger purebred relative.

In some cases, it's unclear which species you might have in hand. After eliminating the chain pickerel from the running (in the absence of chain markings), look again at the sides. If there are plentiful bean-shaped markings, it's a pike. If you see a series of vertical bars—which may be faded, depending on the water and other environmental factors— it's a muskellunge.

For all these species, most anglers concentrate on the larger waters where the fish live during early spring, late summer, and autumn. Big lures, large baitfish, and heavy-duty tackle are standard when pursuing these impressive creatures. Local sports shops can give some suggestions on tackle requirements, boat rentals, any local guides, and places to try.

A general rule of thumb when pike angling is to use baits about one-quarter as long as the fish size you'd like to catch, and this often holds up surprisingly well. Be warned, however: When you start targeting the larger sizes, your strike rate will diminish accordingly. Another factor to consider when seeking the "water wolf"—so called because of its mean-looking teeth and reputation for voracity—is its feeding habits. A northern will often smash a fish or bait sideways, hold it there momentarily, then swim away slowly for an indeterminate distance. It will then stop, turn its victim toward it, and begin the process of swallowing it headfirst. What this means is that after the initial strike, put your reel into free spool (if you're using a spinning reel, open the bail), and let line out as the fish moves away. A few moments after it has stopped moving, engage the reel and set the hook. If you try setting the hook immediately upon detecting the fish, there's a good chance you'll simply snatch the bait away.

Muskellunge angling is practically legendary in its frustration level, but there are some things that can help you increase your success rate. One is timing: More than one bass angler has reported unusual success on muskies on favorite bass lakes early in spring, right after ice-out. Another is tackle—use heavy, sturdy gear and stout line with appropriate leader material, like steel. It's all well and good to hook one of these 20- or 30-pound monsters, but without the right gear it can break off in the same amount of time it takes to yell, "Fish on!"

Another trick to keep in your arsenal is the figure-8 retrieve. It often happens that a muskellunge will be partly interested in your lure, following it toward your boat or shore position. In these cases, as soon as you see the fish, increase your retrieve speed—many anglers have the initial inclination to slow down, which usually just turns the fish off. If you're in a boat and the fish follows the lure all the way in, when you have about two or three rod lengths of line still out, plunge the rod tip into the water and pull the lure through the water such that it describes a figure 8. One guide has told me that nearly a quarter of his hooked muskies are caught using this technique.

Panfish: Sunfish, Perch, Crappie, Bullheads

What kid didn't start out his or her angling career catching sunnies and bullheads from a local pond, lake, or creek? The Garden State has numerous varieties of these from one border to the other: bluegills, pumpkinseed sunfish, redbreast sunfish, green sunfish, yellow perch, white perch, rock bass, white bass, black crappie, white crappie, brown bullheads, and yellow bullheads. Regulations are very liberal—the season is open all year and an angler can keep up to 25 each day for the trophy wall or frying pan (additional restrictions apply to crappie).

The omnipresent sunfish is plentiful through New Jersey, and has launched the fishing careers of innumerable kids.

The majority of these are caught on natural bait, although small lures—jigs, poppers, crankbaits, and even some soft plastics like worms—account for a good portion as well. Summertime is generally best for sunfish and bullheads, although crappie are caught in high numbers in spring and autumn, and yellow perch are a staple of ice fishermen.

As an aside, I usually recommend that newcomers to fly angling spend a few days or weeks concentrating on pond sunfish during spring and summer. This is an excellent way to warm up to fly fishing, as the still water makes casting relatively easy, the fish are very willing biters, and they can provide good introductory experience in hooking and playing fish on fly tackle.

Finally, in today's world of catch-and-release angling, panfish allow an angler to bring home a meal for an excellent repast—without a guilty conscience.

Shad (*Alosa sapidissima*)

Besides the ritual of trout fishing, anglers celebrate another spring event: the annual Delaware River shad run. (There are occasionally rumors of shad in other rivers as well, including the Passaic and Hudson, but these are often unconfirmed.) From late March into June, these anadromous fish come back from the ocean to their native waters and provide outstanding sport to a host of anglers on shore, wading the waters, or in boats.

Short lived as this fishery is, it nevertheless accounts for a hugely disproportionate percentage of the year's Delaware River fishing activity. Small artificials, especially shad darts and flutter spoons, produce most of the fish caught, and some fly enthusiasts do well with subsurface patterns. This "poor man's tarpon" strikes out of reflex during its spawning run, like most species that return from the ocean to spawn, and baits typically come in an assortment of bright colors to catch its attention. Position is critical: Since shad are merely passing through on their way to their ultimate spawning locations, they will not go out of their way, and tend to follow specific routes within the river. If your cast is a mere few feet off, the action will be nonexistent. Move into the hot zone, however, and you could end up with more bites than you know how to handle.

Walleye (*Stizostedion vitreum*)

Despite this fish's popularity in many parts of the United States, the walleye is one of the least utilized fisheries in New Jersey. There are excellent populations in a few waters, like the Delaware River, Swartswood Lake, Lake Hopatcong, and Monksville Reservoir, and developing populations elsewhere in the state, yet most resident freshwater anglers simply don't bother with them . . . leaving more opportunities for you. This is even more mystifying when you realize that the walleye's history in our state is much more extensive than is generally realized: Plenty of attempts to establish populations were being explored about a quarter century ago, and a look through the regulatory archives shows limits and seasons for the "pike-perch"—so called because of its resemblance to both of those species, although it is in fact related only to the yellow perch—dating as far back as 1912.

The walleye is more sensitive to light than most fish, and as a result tends to avoid it assiduously. This means that the fish is usually associated with greater depths, although, as with any other "rule" in fishing, this isn't always so. Many years, especially during late spring, anglers do well using top-water lures for the sometimes enigmatic walleye. It is true that they will move into shallower waters to feed at appropriate times of the day when it's light enough for them to spot forage but not too light for comfort. These times will differ for different bodies of water, depending primarily on turbidity. In general they prefer areas where the bottom is hard, consisting of sand, gravel, and/or rock.

Diet consists predominantly of small fish, but they will also feed on crayfish, small amphibians, leeches, and snails. Natural bait is preferred by many anglers, although jigs, deep-diving crankbaits, and spinners also produce well.

Striped Bass (*Morone saxatilis*)

Striped bass are generally considered in a saltwater context, but there are some worthy freshwater opportunities for this fish in the Garden State. The striper and its hybrid variants can be found in places like the Delaware and Maurice Rivers, Lake Hopatcong, and elsewhere. Hybrids can grow up to 10 pounds, and full-strain stripers of 20, 30, or more pounds will test the mettle of any angler. The freshwater state record for this great fish was 36.5 pounds, caught in 2001 in the Delaware River.

The open season in fresh water is March 1 through December, with a daily limit of two; the first must be between 24 and 28 inches (inclusive) and the second at least 34 inches. (Note that these requirements differ from those governing stripers caught from salt water; consult the current marine-fishing regulations for more details.) Hybrids (crossed with white bass), distinguished from their purebred brethren by the distinctly broken dark lines along their sides, are available year-round and limited to two daily, each at least 16 inches; exceptions apply in the Raritan River downstream of Duke Island Park Dam.

Carp (*Cyprinus carpio*)

Carp are ubiquitous, and can be found in the vast majority of waters throughout the state. Even though they can get huge—the state-record carp is the largest state-record fresh-water fish, period, at 47 pounds—and provide tremendous fights, they don't get the press that many other species do. Doughballs (especially flavored with fruit extracts), worms, and corn kernels account for the majority of these large-scaled leviathans.

They are additionally popular with bow fishermen in early and midspring. During this time they are often found in shallow, nearshore areas, and provide a suitable large target for such missiles. Conventional anglers target them as well, but the carp has a well-deserved reputation for its finicky habits. British anglers have for years specialized in techniques used to catch these worthy battlers. Two components of a suc-cessful approach are chumming the waters before fishing them (depending on local regulations) and using as light a line as you can get away with.

It's worth noting here that carp can provide real surprises every so often. I recall an instance years ago when I was participating in a bass tournament on the upper Hudson River, and my companion and I were working a backwater section. He was throwing a spinnerbait, which is standard fare for largemouth bass, when something huge smashed his lure. During the fight that ensued, his eyes were shining and his face was stuck in a huge grin; undoubtedly he was sure he'd be bringing home the day's "lunker" prize (biggest single fish of the tournament), and perhaps even a state record. Yep, you guessed it—a big ol' carp had snatched his spinnerbait. This is one of the great joys of fishing: There's no telling what might happen.

Channel Catfish (*Ictalurus punctatus*)

If you like big, hard-fighting underdogs, try for one of the local channel catfish. These can exceed 30 pounds in our state, although you're more likely to see individuals of 5 to 10 pounds, and they will attack a huge range of baits and lures. Unlike the catfish stereotype, which portrays them as dull-witted, slow-moving eaters of crud relegated to muck- or mud-bottomed depths, channel catfish are sleek, fast-moving opportunistic feeders that will gladly chase down an artificial bait. Just ask state-record holder Howard Hudson (if you can find him), who took his 33-pounder with a Mepps Black Fury spinner in 1978.

The channel cat is easily distinguished from its smaller bullhead brethren by the deeply forked tail and (in most cases) a collection of randomly placed small brown dots on its sides. Popular baits include chicken livers, chunks of hot dogs, gobs of nightcrawlers, and baitfish. Those who prefer to hoodwink them with something made of metal or plastic use crankbaits, jigs, and spinners or spinnerbaits. They are equally at home in slower-moving sections of larger rivers and in still waters (ponds, reservoirs, and lakes).

2

BOATING

BOATING AND FISHING go together like Laurel and Hardy (or, for the younger ones out there, maybe Ren and Stimpy). At times it's difficult to imagine one without the other, and New Jersey is no exception. Although there are plenty of shoreline opportunities throughout the state (see the next chapter), there are invariably times when some of the prime locations will simply be out of reach of the landbound angler. Another factor to consider is casting direction: Often the same nearshore area is better worked from the water side rather than the land side, simply because the direction in which the retrieve occurs can trigger strikes that might otherwise be missed.

It's important to realize that, although our state has no shortage of fresh waters in which plenty of gamefish may be found, there is very little in the way of huge waters like those reservoirs and impoundments so common in the South, or huge raging rivers such as those found out west. This means that in most cases, you can get by with minimal nautical equipment.

For the sake of simplicity, I've broken this discussion into three sections: rivers and streams, still waters, and big waters.

Rivers and Streams

Most of New Jersey's rivers and streams are small flows that meander harmlessly through the landscape. Many times the entire width of the water can be handled easily with some skilled casting, but for those occasions on which the far shore might be just beyond reach, or you'd like to cover a larger stretch than you could on foot, a number of options are available.

Among the simplest is a canoe. Lightweight, easily transported, and painless to operate, models can be as small as 11 or so feet in length, weighing less than 60 pounds. These are perfect for exploring small rivers that might offer limited access points for much of their flow. Such a canoe will strap easily onto almost any automobile, allows you plenty of room for your rod (or rods) and other tackle, and can handle minimal water depths with ease. A number of varieties have a modified stern design that allows the use of a small motor, should that be your preference.

Another good option is a johnboat, although these vessels will seem more cumbersome on the smaller river and stream stretches you might plan to fish. They also tend to be heavier than canoes, an important consideration when transporting or portaging the boat (see below).

A more modern approach is the kayak. Good for those who wish to stay very lightweight, this option allows for some minimalist fishing using a single rod-and-reel combo with a bare-bones assortment of tackle. It has the advantage of being able to get to some places that are difficult, if not impossible, to reach via other methods, and it will test your skill as an angler to an usual degree, forcing you to make the most of the little you have with you.

Some people have reported success with small inflatable craft; I recommend that you look into this very carefully before trying. Rivers are notorious for having unpredictable bottoms, with rapidly changing depths and plenty of stickups along the way, any of which can compromise the integrity of whatever material your craft is made of.

An important factor to keep in mind is weight. You will have to get your craft on and off your car, and you may also need to portage it past any obstructions on the river. These might include extremely shallow runs, or a spot choked with laydowns. Be sure to keep your boat and equipment complement to a level you can handle, either by yourself or with your partner, as the case may be.

It's generally easier to navigate a river stretch if you have a partner and a second vehicle. The drill goes as follows: The two of you ride in tandem to the takeout point (the place you plan on ending the day's activities), with the boat on either vehicle. One vehicle is parked there; then both parties drive with the boat and all the equipment to the launch point. At the trip's conclusion, the two parties can either load up the other vehicle (already parked there) and drive back to the starting point to pick up the first car, or drive immediately to Point A, pick up that car, and bring both vehicles back to Point B to load and divide up the equipment as desired.

If you can't find a companion, it's still possible to embark on a solo river trip. Use a bicycle as the second vehicle and pack it in your car with everything else. Chain the bike to a tree or other immovable object (preferably out of sight) at the trip's endpoint, and drive to the starting point. At trip's end, keep your boat and equipment out of sight as well as you can, bike back to your car, and go get your stuff.

Lakes, Reservoirs, and Large Ponds

Garden State still waters are typically between 20 and a few hundred surface acres in size. Another truism throughout much of the state is limitations on outboard motor types and sizes: Many waters allow no motors, and most that do allow them permit only electric outboards. And among the relatively few remaining bodies, the vast majority require 9.9 horsepower or less. (In fact, according to my count, there are only seven waters throughout the Garden State that allow unlimited horsepower usage, and of those, only two—Lake Hopatcong and Greenwood Lake, discussed under "Big Waters" below—are really big enough to make the larger motor necessary.)

This leads to the inescapable conclusion that almost any small craft capable of taking a small electric or gasoline motor will serve well on the vast majority of waters you're likely to be fishing. A johnboat, V-hull, or even canoe will in many cases fit the bill nicely. It might be worth your while to stay on the small side, as quite a large number of launch areas cannot easily accommodate a trailer. It's necessary, of course, to balance the conflict of small-and-easily-handled versus bigger-and-more-comfortable against the kinds of waters you expect to be fishing.

The option that works best for me is a small johnboat with an electric motor on the majority of my boating excursions. In those relatively rare cases where something bigger is really necessary, I either glom onto a friend who's appropriately equipped, or go with local boat and motor rentals.

Big Waters

New Jersey's three big waters are Lake Hopatcong, Greenwood Lake, and the Delaware River. Boating on any of these requires a fairly serious boat with equally serious motor. If you haven't already made the investment in money, time, and emotional energy for a sufficiently powerful boat and motor, consider that if you go this route and confine your fishing to New Jersey, these three waters will comprise nearly half of your fishable waters—unless you also do some salt-water fishing and boating, and that's a whole new discussion outside the purview of this book.

Remember also that the 9.9-horsepower engine, allowed on a fair number of waters in the state, will nearly double the number of waters on which you can legally use the outboard, and can still get you from place to place on these big waters reasonably efficiently.

3

SHORELINE ANGLING AND WADING

A **LTHOUGH MANY ANGLERS** can't imagine fishing without a boat, the opportunities for a sportsman equipped with merely a pair of waders or hip boots are practically limitless. There is definitely something to be said for being able to travel fast and light. Anglers on the road who keeps their car trunk stocked with a couple of rods and reels, a basic tackle selection, and boots or waders can stop and fish at a huge number of spots along the way.

Too, there are plenty of moving water stretches that are essentially unreachable by watercraft, not to mention any number of lentic waters that are walk-in only, making a boat a moot point unless you're willing to carry something in for what is sometimes an exhaustingly (especially if you're carrying a boat!) long distance. Shoreline fishing, or wading directly into the environment, is a simpler and less complicated means of getting to your quarry. And few experiences can beat the elemental feeling of standing in the water while wrestling a stubborn trout or cranky bass.

Even if you don't plan on wading in, it's prudent to have available a pair of calf- or knee-high rubber boots. Areas immediately adjacent to the water tend to be wet at best, and downright (sometimes hazardously) muddy at worst.

Another useful set of footwear is an old pair of sneakers or the like—something that's comfortable and more or less disposable. These are perfect for "wet wading" on scorching summertime days—walking right into the water wearing just your shorts and what my high school marching band leader called "mudders" (shoes for tramping though mud and muck). Fishing and cooling off together is a marvelous way to seek spiritual and physical comfort simultaneously.

Not sure whether to choose hip boots or chest waders? I strongly recommend you keep a pair of each available, for a few reasons. It's sometimes difficult to know which one will serve you better, until you've actually arrived at your target water for the day. Too, either one of these garments will almost certainly spring a leak or two sooner or later, and it's handy to have the other one present as a backup. Also worth considering are those occasions when you have a companion with you, and (depending on similarity in foot size) he or she can join you if you have that second option available. Finally, there's the issue of sole type (more on this in a minute)—if you have hip boots with lug soles, get waders with felt soles. Or vice versa.

Sole type can make a measurable difference in your wading experience. Lug soles tend to be less expensive and

In many locations, wading can get you close to lots of good action, like this respectable largemouth bass hooked from a northern New Jersey pond.

are useful for bottoms that aren't too rocky: mud, sand, silt, gravel, or weeds. On rocky bottoms, felt soles really shine by providing much better traction than lug soles, which tend to slide right off. It's possible to use felt for all bottom surfaces, but I have found that frequent use over softer bottoms tends to get the "interstitial" areas within the felt clogged; they end up less effective on those rocks when you finally do need them there.

A few more odds and ends to consider when shoreline fishing and/or wading:

- In general, try to avoid casting directly in front of you, perpendicular to the shoreline, too much. Angle or fan out your casts to cover more water and get closer to shoreline-based cover or structure where the fish are probably more likely to be holding. (Being directly in the water makes this easier.)

- Safety should be near the forefront of your mind all the time, and especially when you are moving from one position to another. There are essentially two hazards to consider that could lead to drowning or other physical injury. The first is water movement, in particular swift current. Try to keep both feet in contact with the bottom at all times, and use a shuffling gait when moving; this helps you maintain better balance and also alerts you more quickly if you encounter a sudden change in depth. And when you're moving, keep your body oriented such that the imaginary line between your two feet is parallel to the direction of the current, making it tougher for the water to knock you over.

  The second hazard is soft mud. I vividly recall an instance a couple of years ago when I was wading around the periphery of a small pond in Morris County while trying for largemouths and pickerel (I did manage a couple of the latter). At one point I was standing on firm bottom, and then took a step—one single step—into slightly deeper water. In two blinks of an eye I found myself chest-deep in mud. I was fortunate that it hadn't been any deeper, or drowning would have been a real possibility. It took me close to an hour to extricate myself, none the worse for wear but with a greatly sobered perspective. Be wary of these danger spots.

• One of the inconveniences of wading is the ubiquitous problem of your pant legs riding up when you're donning chest waders or hip boots. A simple solution is to tuck your pant legs into your socks before pulling on the boots or waders. No, this won't work if you're wearing short pants, but I find it intolerably uncomfortable to wear shorts under wading gear anyway.

• A useful piece of equipment when you're this close to the water is a pair of polarized sunglasses. These go a long way in cutting through the surface glare, enabling you to more easily examine the underwater lay of the land, and often to spot the fish themselves.

4

TACKLE CONSIDERATIONS

CONVENIENT AS IT might sound, you can't effectively chase every freshwater gamefish species in New Jersey with a single set of equipment. Dunking worms for bluegills is an entirely different pastime than throwing an oversized lure for a muskellunge. What follows are some approaches that should serve you well.

Small Species: Panfish, Stream Trout, and Smallmouths

Although there are individual trout and smallmouths that will test light gear to the utmost, the majority of specimens you encounter will readily succumb to ultralight or light tackle. Besides, if you hook that next brook trout record while using 2-pound test on a wisp of a rod, think of the fun you'll have.

An excellent all-around combo would be the ubiquitous spinning rod and reel—preferably a pair that is well matched. Getting a matching rod and reel is easy: Either purchase the two as a package kit or solicit recommendations from the tackle store salesclerk, who will be glad to help you. A medium- to good-quality monofilament line of about 6-pound test will serve nicely.

Terminal tackle will center on hooks. Trout and panfish anglers should stay small, using hook sizes around 8 and smaller, while those seeking smallmouths can get away with hooks up to size 1 or so. If natural baits are your method of choice, then baitholder hooks (which have additional barbs along the shank) can be useful. Anybody using soft plastic baits for smallies can try worm hooks, characterized by the right-angled turns in the shank, near the eye.

An assortment of floats and weights can round out the terminal tackle. Swivels, snaps, and combo units (called—appropriately enough—snap swivels) have their use as well.

Medium Species: Largemouths, Walleye, Pickerel, Pike, Shad, and Catfish

Some of the species in this and the next category—large species—might really fit into either. For example, the rank-and-file carp that you're likely to encounter will be somewhere in the 2- to 6-pound range and will be handled very satisfactorily by the equipment described here. But there is also an abundance of much larger carp, with poundage well into double digits, and if you're specifically targeting those big guys, you'd be well advised to bump up your tackle accordingly.

Because of the great popularity of bass fishing, equipment designed for largemouths is an excellent place to start. It's readily available, comes in a variety of styles and designs to handle different styles of bassin', and can generally be easily adapted to fishing for other species.

There are two basic styles available: baitcasting and spinning gear. Both have their advantages and disadvantages. With baitcasting reels, the spool spins as the line comes off during casting, mandating close control over the reel's behavior. Lack of attention to this during casting will almost invariably result in the spool turning too quickly for the line to come off efficiently, and the result is the classic bird's nest, a terrible snarl that in the worst cases will require you to take a knife or scissors to the mess. Learning to thumb the reel properly while casting is an essential skill for use of this equipment.

Once mastered, however, baitcasting gear has significant advantages over spinning equipment. Line twist (see the discussion of spinning gear, below) is essentially nonexistent, casting of dense or heavy lures is much easier, accurate casting is simplified, and the equipment in general is hardier and can take more of a beating—an important quality to have when trying to muscle in that once-in-a-lifetime trophy you unexpectedly hooked.

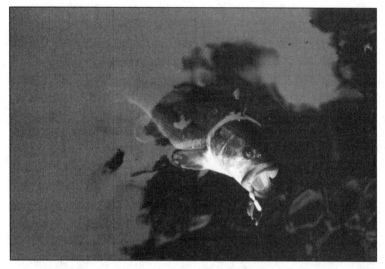

Largemouth bass are virtually ubiquitous in New Jersey's waters. This one fell for a small spinnerbait.

Having said that, spinning gear has its proponents as well, and serious bass anglers own both. Spinning reels are much easier to learn to cast and tend to be less expensive; moreover, an individual reel can usually be switched from left- to right-handed. (Baitcasting reels are one or the other and can't be switched on the fly.)

Whichever way you go, be sure that the rod you select is appropriate for the reel, as baitcasting and spinning rods have different designs; the one simply can't be used for the other reel type. Just as important, be sure that the weight and strength of the rod are appropriate for the reel you've selected.

If you have any questions on this, stick with prematched combo packages or, again, ask the salesclerk for assistance.

Once you get into medium-weight gear, line options start to open up. Monofilament was king for many years, but nowadays you can opt for braided line or the new fluorocarbons. The latter has some significant advantages over nylon monofilament, but also costs more and requires more attention to certain details of equipment selection and maintenance. All things considered, a decent nylon monofilament is an excellent choice for practically all types of angling.

Yet even within this niche there are plenty of options: stiff (abrasion resistant) versus limp (easier casting, less line twist), and clear versus colored are but two of the choices. Use your common sense and whatever advice you can glean from trusted friends or sales staff to guide you. Given the fish sizes you are likely to encounter, and the environment you'll be fishing, line strength should be somewhere in the 8- to 17-pound-test area.

Okay, I've mentioned line twist a few times; let's take this opportunity to discuss it more. When line is retrieved after casting, a spinning reel's bail wraps the line around the stationary spool with its circular gathering motion, imparting some twist to the line. Left to its own devices, this twist will continue to accumulate, and sooner or later it will reach a point at which the line can no longer tolerate it. The result will be sudden, unexpected tangles in the line, especially when you cast.

When this happens, it's high time to untwist the line. If you're in a boat, remove all terminal tackle from the line, and slowly pay line out into the water while you move the boat forward. After you have enough cast-lengths of line out, simply retrieve the line and continue fishing. If you're in or nearing moving water, you can do the same thing by letting the current take your line out. If you're shorebound next to still water, be sure to have a swivel tied to the end of your line, and a lure or hook affixed to the swivel. Anchor the hook/lure to a tree or other similar stationary object and walk away from the anchor, letting out line as you go. When you're a sufficient distance from the end of the line, set the bail and exert some pressure on the line, letting the swivel spin and allowing the twists to come out.

Large Species: Muskellunge, Striped Bass, Lake Trout

If you're going bear hunting, you'd best be armed for bear. The same thing is true in fishing: If you're targeting fish that are likely to be big and strong, it's important to be ready for them.

Although it's possible to use spinning gear for these guys, and in fact some very successful anglers do, the fact is that baitcasting gear is superior for seeking and bringing in those grunt-while-you-play-them monsters dwelling in our waters. As discussed in the previous category, baitcasting tackle tends to withstand abuse (and these big fish *will* abuse the equipment, believe me) more readily, and enables you to sling large lures or baits repeatedly, with greater distance and accuracy as well as less fatigue. General approaches for ensuring a matched rod and reel, already discussed, apply here as well.

Even if you refuse to give up your beloved spinning gear, however, you needn't pass up these big fish. Manufacturers do provide spinning products for this niche, and you can also use spinning equipment designed for saltwater applications.

Don't skimp on line strength. I have fished with one of New Jersey's very best muskellunge anglers (who also offers guiding services), and he regularly uses 100-pound-test line for these large, powerful fish. It's unlikely, of course, that you'll see a specimen of even half that weight, but it's good to have the extra heft to deal with the sudden surges, line-unfriendly obstacles that invariably interfere with your fishing efforts, and other stresses involved in chasing fish of this magnitude.

Hook size is an important consideration. Small hooks simply don't have enough of a bite to securely grab these fellows, and could in fact unbend or break off too readily. Look for appropriate styles in the 1/0 to 5/0 range for best results.

Other Considerations and Accessories

In no particular order, here are some items that will enhance your fishing experiences.

Lures

Those who eschew natural baits often never look back, and in fact there are plenty of cases when a properly chosen and well-presented artificial will greatly outfish the real thing. Size and style depend, of course, on the target species, but a wise angler will start to amass a collection using most of the following: crankbaits (surface, sinking, and diving), spinnerbaits, in-line spinners, spoons, soft plastics (worms, jerkbaits, creatures, tubes, plus any of the nearly limitless variety that this class offers), jigs, and anything else that could be promising.

Flies

If you'll be fly fishing, then it goes without saying that you'll need a collection of flies (although I've met more than one angler who baits tiny hooks with natural bait and uses fly gear to present it). There's hardly a species of fish that can't be taken in this manner . . . though some are more commonly pursued than others, of course. In any event, be sure to have the major classes of fly well represented: dry flies, wet flies, nymphs, and streamers.

Stringer

In today's world of catch-and-release, the practice of which is critical for maintaining most of our fisheries, talking about any means of keeping or killing fish in some circles is not only politically incorrect, but downright blasphemous. Yet the fact remains that in plenty of places, the existing fishery is managed to easily withstand controlled removal of a part of the population. In some cases, this actually benefits the fishery.

There are two types of stringer: the poly stringer, usually with a ring on one end and a spikelike metal piece on the other, and the chain stringer, which is a length of chain to which a number of metal clips are affixed. The poly kind can be used with almost any fish, but if you wish to keep your catch immersed and as healthy as possible before its final removal from the water, then a chain stringer is preferable. The fish will keep better if you slip the clip through the lower jaw rather than through the gill area. If, on the other hand, you're dealing with very large fish (say, you want to bring that 20-pound northern pike home), then the poly stringer is pretty much your best option.

Wading Vest

If wading makes up a significant part of your angling activity, a wading vest is de rigueur. There are innumerable small items that you need at your beck and call when angling, and if you're knee-deep in water with your hands occupied with the rod and reel, how else will you keep all that stuff with you?

Camera

No, this won't help you catch fish, but it will help you capture the moment. CPR (catch, photo, and release) is an excellent way to help maintain fish populations that need protection, while at the same time allowing you take something home besides just another fish story. I consider a camera to be an essential part of any fishing trip.

Net

Useful when wading, boating, or shoreline angling, a net often makes the difference between a successful landing and an escaped fish. Too, it can save you from an unexpected hooking (ask experienced bass anglers if they've ever hooked themselves trying to lip a bass!) and often allows for less wear and tear on the fish itself, increasing its survival chances if you plan on releasing it.

Waders

See the chapter "Shoreline Angling and Wading," for detailed information on waders.

Tackle Storage

There has been a veritable explosion in tackle box design in recent years. You can select varying sizes, hard or soft containers, go with modular approaches (using interchangeable trays for different classes of gear) . . . the list goes on. Serious anglers have multiple systems. For example, I have one system for saltwater angling; another for bass, pickerel, and walleye angling; one for trout; and another for everything else. Decide on the likely amount of stuff you want to carry around with you, and the styles that suit you best, before making your choices.

Fishfinders

There are many boating situations in which effective implementation of a fishfinder can mean the difference between nonstop action—and the exact opposite. Some models are designed for permanent installation, while others are highly portable. Which kind to get? Factors governing decisions like this include how often you'll be boating, your willingness to do the installation, and cost.

Other

Any of the following items can enhance your fishing experience. Having too much simply results in clutter; it's up to you to find the proper balance. Many anglers swear by lure scents, line clippers, a multipurpose tool, a small flashlight, spare oil or grease for your reels, devices to measure or weigh any fish you catch, hemostats or pliers, extra spools of line, a line straightener (when fly fishing), repair parts for waders or their soles, and anything else that you decide you can't live without.

5

TAKE A KID FISHING

ROD AND REEL, check. Tackle box and contents, check. License, check. Bait, check. Kid . . . where is that guy, anyway?

It's been said that the greatest gift you can give your children is time. And what better way to share time is there than fishing? It provides a common purpose. Throw in skills learned, conservation lessons absorbed, and appreciation for the outdoors gained, and you have a winning combination. Besides, you'll probably learn a little bit more about each other.

Few outdoor activities are as satisfying or rewarding as family fishing trips. Even if you aren't an experienced angler, it's surprisingly easy to teach the fundamentals to youngsters, and it's just possible that you'll give them a hobby, and an appreciation for our natural resources, that can last a lifetime.

Any fishing time together is better than none, but there are definite ways to maximize the value of the time you do invest in this activity. Probably the most useful guideline for success can be borrowed from the Cub Scouts: KISMIF (keep it simple, make it fun).

Let's look at keeping it simple. First and foremost, make sure that children's equipment is well within their ability. For much younger kids, a good way to go is to simply have a sturdy rod made out of cane, bamboo, synthetics, what have you, with no reel. It should be no longer than the kids can comfortably handle, with an equal length of reasonably strong—at least 10-pound-test—line tied to the end. Add a small hook, bobber, and live bait, and they're ready to start dunking for panfish, bullhead catfish, or even stocked trout. For bait, you can't go wrong with worms or bread balls.

For somewhat older juniors, a simple spincasting rod-and-reel combination is great. (These are readily identified by the closed-face spincast reel, with a push button.) For a modest purchase price, you can get a complete combo, pre-spooled with fishing line, which will be more than adequate for a couple of years. If they (or you) have never used one before, take 20 minutes in the backyard to let them become familiar with their operation—these reels are fairly easy to master. Add the hook, bobber, and bait, and you're ready to go.

Select a nearby spot, and keep the drive short; there's no need to drive cross-country. There are invariably a number of spots close by where catching fish is a good bet. If you're not familiar with them, check with New Jersey Division of Fish and Wildlife or your local department of parks and recreation. Don't overlook any water as a possibility, as long as it's legal. My sons and I have even caught goldfish—big ones, too—out of a local suburban pond.

The last part of KISMIF is making it fun. Easy enough, if you follow a few basic rules. First, let your kids do as much as they can or want to on their own. If they need help, they'll ask. Let them have their own failures as well as their own successes. You can always ask them if they need help, but don't force it on them.

Next, don't expect to spend a great deal of time fishing. Two hours is the outer limit for many kids, even if they're having nonstop action. Break up the activity, or simply plan on doing other things as well.

Be sure to attend to their creature comforts. Dress should be appropriate for the weather (including sunscreen for sunny days), and keep those drinks and snacks available.

Where to go? The best first choice is the municipal park closest to you that includes fishing water. This will have a number of advantages. It's close by, access will be easy, and there will be plenty to do there if the fishing action is slow or kids tire of angling due to that clan's infamously short attention span. There are many such places described in the main chapters of this book; if none of them seems convenient, contact your local sporting goods store for some advice.

Once your new companions have showed enough staying power to deal with fishing in a focused manner, try escalating the effort level a notch or two. This can take any of the following forms: going boating in a pond or small lake, visiting a place that has a longer hike in before reaching water's edge, graduating to artificial lures, and the like. These kind of excursions increase the reward-to-exertion ratio, intensifying the sense of victory that young anglers experiences while at the same time strengthening the bond between you. I do, however, recommend that you attempt these escalations only after allowing kids to experience some unencumbered angling.

By the way, don't let any of those old lingering stereotypes stop you—fishing is by no means only a male pastime these days. I know mothers who take their sons fishing, fathers who take their daughters . . . Angling is for everybody. What if you don't have your own kid to take? Don't let that stop you. Get permission and borrow a friend's kid—maybe the one whose parents don't have the time or inclination to go themselves.

6

NORTHERN NEW JERSEY PONDS, LAKES, AND RESERVOIRS

Bergen County

Bear Swamp Lake

If ever there was a fishing spot in suburban New Jersey where you can combine angling with aerobic exercise, this is it. Remote location and foot-only accessibility make this lake an excellent choice for those seeking some solitude within the wilds of Bergen County, but it's recommended only for those who don't mind the long walk in—and out—as well as the cardiovascular workout while negotiating the lake itself.

Lush and plentiful lily pad coverage will dictate much of the direction your lure and equipment selection will take. While this place screams *largemouth bass*, they often don't come as readily to your baits as you might like. Plentiful pickerel are mixed in, although the pickings for these snakelike predators have ebbed somewhat in recent years. Channel catfish are the other large gamefish present, and there are lots of panfish in the forms of sunfish, crappie, and yellow perch.

For lure selection, go weedless all the way for the bass and chain pickerel; good choices include a Mann's Rat, Strike King Grass Frog, or Johnson Silver Minnow weedless spoon (preferably with a grub trailer). Texas-rigged worms with a substantial bullet weight are good for getting offerings into the pad openings, and hefty (12-pound or better) abrasion-resistant line paired with a good stiff rod is key. Standard natural bait rigs will work fine for the catfish and panfish. To avoid weed-related headaches, try fishing during early spring and autumn, but expect more pickerel than bass at those times.

The primary obstacle here is getting in with your stuff. Although I've never measured the distance, I estimate that it is at least 0.5 mile. It works best if you have a single rod, tackle vest, and waders (better to carry the waders unless the boots are unusually comfortable). It's also prudent to tote along some drinking water and a small snack or two. Other options include a float tube, or coming with a canoe and a strong friend. The latter approach might be helped by using a dolly made for the purpose—just be aware that much of the walk is uphill. Although I've never tried, bicycling in might be an option as well.

Go to Route 202 (Ramapo Valley Road) in Mahwah. About a mile north of the southern Mahwah boundary, look for Bear Swamp Road and Marion Drive; park on the latter. Get all your equipment together, walk across the road and the Ramapo River onto Bear Swamp Road, and follow the walk-in-access-only road to get to the lake.

Ramapo Lake

Part of the Ramapo River system, Ramapo Lake is surrounded by a combination of wooded areas and private residences. It's located in the Ramapo Mountain State Forest, which encompasses nearly 2,400 acres.

Although there is a road providing access to the lake, it is open only to "authorized traffic." Others may enter, but by nonmotorized means only. This, of course, puts severe restrictions on the methods you may use to angle here, for the distance to the lake via access road is nearly a mile. Unfortunately, the roadway is fairly hilly, and—as at least one tired angler has remarked—"You could have cardiac arrest trying to walk back up the road."

The water, which used to be much smaller before the construction of a small dam, was formerly known as "Rotten Pond." A likely explanation for this unusual-sounding name is that the area's early Dutch settlers referred to it as Rote (rat) Pond, referring to the muskrat population.

There is plenty of shoreline access, but if you'd like to escape from the confines of land, you'll have to bring in whatever vessel you can by hand and foot. If you and your partner are in good enough shape, you can carry in a canoe or small rowboat that distance; however, an excellent solution for the access situation is the use of a float tube, which can be hefted in slung over your shoulder.

The two primary species you'll probably be targeting are bass and chain pickerel, so good lure choices include topwater lures (Zara Spooks, buzzbaits, poppers); some lures for lily pad surfaces, like weedless frogs and spoons; and any other types that you favor—good choices include plastic worms, soft plastic jerkbaits, crankbaits, and spinnerbaits.

By late summer, the weed growth is substantial, as are the beds of lily pads. Both types of areas are worthwhile starting places. Other spots worth trying are shallow areas near shore, with deep water close by. If bass or pickerel aren't your preference, species that will respond to smaller lures (or hooks tipped with some worm) include bluegills, yellow perch, crappie, and bullheads.

During cooler weather, concentrating on the pickerel should pay dividends; as the calendar turns to winter, fishermen do well on pickerel and perch, especially through the ice.

To reach the lake, follow Route 287 to West Oakland Avenue in Oakland, and look for a parking lot on the left side of the road marked with a sign for the Ramapo Mountain State Forest. You can park here and follow a trail in, or continue a bit farther down the road to another small parking area on the left, where the unmarked road leads into the woods to the lake.

Scarlet Oak Pond

Of the two public-access still waters associated with Ramapo Valley Reservation, this one—although the smaller of the duet—is easier to get to and easier to fish, accounting for much greater fishing pressure. Nevertheless, the fish will respond to your baits much of the time.

Anglers are essentially confined to shoreline angling, and the primary target varieties are largemouth bass, sunfish, and catfish. The 22-acre pond has depths up to 50 feet, concentrated in the western half of the water. The majority of the pond's easily accessed shores (there is a relative lack of thickly grown trees or brush) abuts gently sloping shallow sections; look for the sharper drop-offs along the western shore. During spring and summer, sunfish and smaller bass are fairly evenly distributed throughout the shallower waters, and some of the larger bass (I've seen them up to about 3 pounds) may be found in areas closer to the steep drop-offs.

The water has very low visibility and is subject to substantial algal blooms by midsummer, so select baits that can easily be seen or tracked by your quarry. Small to medium in-line spinners will attract bass and larger sunnies, and carefully worked spinnerbaits can grab some of the more mature guys. In both cases, be sure the spinning blades are nice and shiny. I prefer silver to gold; if you prefer something with more subtle action, weedless worms or other plastics can work, but make sure they have some bright color or don't stay motionless too long.

Those using natural baits for sunfish or bass are advised to twitch the offering every so often, to add some additional visual appeal to the smell attractant. Catfish anglers can be confident that the whiskered dwellers within can find the proffered worm/liver/stinkbait without difficulty.

Along the more-difficult-access areas that are more heavily wooded, you'll find a number of paths cut through the lumber. If you're willing to sidestep these paths and make your way through the wooded areas to pondside, thereby reaching small stretches that have been less pressured, you will be increasing your likelihood of success at least a few percentage points.

Access is a snap. Drive in along Route 202, in the north-eastern part of Bergen County, to Mahwah. The reservation parking lot is on the western side of the road, easily spotted by a large Smokey Bear sign listing that day's fire hazard. Park your vehicle and walk in via the paved pathway. Cross the Ramapo River via the footbridge, and you'll reach the south side of the pond within a minute or two.

Essex County

Branch Brook Park Pond

Branch Brook Park in Newark is well known for reasons besides fishing, such as its magnificent cherry trees and its famous designers, the Olmsted Brothers. But starting in April, local anglers have other things on their mind.

As with many waters in the Garden State, the season kicks off with trout. The Division of Fish and Wildlife supplies a veritable bonanza of hatchery produce to this lake—over 2,000 salmonids are added each spring. Look for them in the more southern part of the lake, between Park and Orange Streets. It has a more pronounced deep-water section (even if it's only about 8 feet deep) than does the northern area, providing an environment more conducive to the comfort of these cold-water dwellers.

This section of the lake is deceptively wide, with the trout's most desirable habitat right smack in the middle. This means that long casts are critical to your success. Use whatever means you have for those distance casts: Having a reel in good working order, an adequate amount of line on the spool, smooth and nick-free line guide linings, a long rod, and light line will all help. If you need to, add a little extra weight to the complement of terminal tackle (one or two split shot will probably suffice). Use of the right float can help as well; some models are denser and more aerodynamically efficient than others.

When the trout activity starts to die off, try the other, northern stretch of the lake, past Park Street, and check out the largemouth bass action. Soft plastics like jerkbaits and worms in muted colors, small spinnerbaits, and jigs with trailers are good starting methods. If using a jerkbait, work it at a moderate speed at first, and slow down as you explore a particular area. If you need to stay down in the depths, affix a small weight to the line about 8 inches in front of the lure. Worm action seems most effective with little or no added weight.

Don't be too surprised if you hook into the occasional crappie while you're searching for largemouths: Specimens up to a pound have been reported from here. And if you get tired of flinging your trout rig as far as you can, relax a little and fish closer to shore. The ever-present bluegill population will be glad to grab whatever trout bait you happen to be using. Channel catfish and bullheads are also present; these feline look-alikes can be enticed with savory gobs of nightcrawlers or liver (chicken or beef), fished on the bottom of the deeper sections. Carp have been reported from these waters, but the population may not be as stable as it once was.

One approach is via Interstate 280 eastbound, into the area of Clifton Avenue and Orange Street. From the north, Route 21 leads directly into McCarter Highway; from there, wend your way (using a map) west to Park Avenue. Cross over the lake, and turn right onto the park lane.

Grover Cleveland Park Pond

It's small, it's in the middle of suburban sprawl, and it's the color of chocolate milk. But an angler can have a field day in the fields of Grover Cleveland Park in Caldwell and Essex Fells.

Bass anglers have plenty of opportunity to hook into some willing biters here. Don't be surprised to find that a good number of 10- to 14-inch bass will come to your hand, if you follow some commonsense guidelines. First of all, keep in mind the water quality. It's very discolored, with low visibility—you need to help the bass find your offering. Make sure that it's brightly colored, and/or makes a fair amount of vibration or flash in the water. I've had luck with spinnerbaits, Rat-L-Traps, and curly-tailed plastic worms with a splash of red or chartreuse.

The section of the pond near the field house is relatively shallow, while the opposite side, near the parking area, drops off more quickly into deeper water. Plan your strategy accordingly.

Go ahead and bring your kids; try setting them up with small hooks and panfish baits (earthworms, mealworms, bread balls) near the drainpipe just around the pond's corner from the field house. Actually, that whole length of shoreline (opposite the trees) is often inhabited by plenty of hungry bluegills.

If you've had chicken for dinner recently, bring the leftover liver, put it on a medium-sized hook, add some weight, and cast it right to the bottom of the deepest part of the pond. Also, bring a good book. But make sure the book isn't too engrossing, because you'll need to notice when your line starts moving to one side or the other. When it does, put the book down, pick up your rod, set the hook—and hang on. The channel catfish you may well have hooked won't come in without a fight.

To complete the repertoire of gamefish available from this little pond (you can walk around its entire periphery in just a few minutes), there is the omnipresent carp. They make themselves clearly visible during the warmer-weather months, paddling about near the surface as though they haven't a care in the world. Corn kernels, worms, and dough-balls—with some patience—are the tickets for these guys.

To get there, follow Bloomfield Avenue into the Caldwells. Turn onto Roseland Avenue, and right at Runnymede Road. The park, with its small parking area, will soon be on your right.

Verona Park Lake

Although Verona Park might not satisfy your yen for isolated solitude, it will satisfy your desire to feel a fish with fight on the end of your line. With healthy populations of bass, sunfish, carp, catfish, and trout (during the spring stocking), there's something here for almost everyone.

Trout are available from the season opener through May and into June, concentrated near the boathouse—you'll see the other anglers already set up. Most folks put a mealworm on a small bait hook, place a bobber about 18 inches above it, and cast as far as they can toward the center of the lake. Fishermen wielding spinners and small crayfish-imitating crankbaits fool a number of salmonids as well.

Bass fishermen would do well to give this lake its proper due. There's a healthy population of largemouth bass here, and the angler can probe a good variety of visible, fishable structure. Concentrate on the best two times of day: early morning, and late day approaching evening. Because you'll be constrained to a good amount of casting parallel to shore, wading is essential to attain proper casting angles in many areas. No need to feel self-conscious; the dog walkers and bicyclists won't even give you a glance. Start with the faster, aggressive patterns (like crankbaits, spinnerbaits or in-line

Multiple generations of anglers taking advantage of the spring trout angling to be had at Verona Lake Park.

spinners, and rattling crankbaits), and slow down as necessary to finesse baits such as plastic worms and soft jerkbaits. And consider the relative lack of water clarity; give the bass something they can home in on. If it seems that worms are the key, use ones with some bright color.

After trout and bass, catfish and bullheads are probably the next most popular gamefish in this lake. The Division of Fish and Wildlife has included Verona Park as part of its channel cat program since 1987, and more than one practitioner has felt the tug of one of these bewhiskered gamesters. Bullheads are sometimes taken unexpectedly by those seeking trout and sunfish with their nightcrawler or mealworm, especially when the offering is kept on the bottom. For the larger specimens, try sinking a chunk of liver or a mass of nightcrawlers in the deeper sections. And, as with most catfish waters, after-dark angling accounts for a large share of fish.

While most of the springtime anglers are concentrating on trout, some other savvy fishermen have departed from the crowd and are plying the shallow section (near the footbridge) with carp baits. They know what they're doing, for some very hefty specimens—as much as 20 pounds—have been wrestled from this lake. Most of the typical carp baits have produced here, including corn and any of the various dough baits sweetened with honey, fruit extract, or the like.

Panfish abound as well. Bring the kids (or not, if you want the action to yourself), rig up old reliable—the earthworm—and have a ball. Keep the tackle light, keep the approach simple, and keep reeling those scrappy fellers in. The park is located at the corner of Bloomfield Avenue and Lakeside Avenue in Verona; you can't miss the lake in the center.

Hudson County

Lincoln Park Lake
Carp are probably the biggest attraction here. Literally. Some of the big-scaled denizens of this modest 3-acre municipal

pond reach toward double-digit size, and you can occasionally find some cousins of the carp here in redoubtable size as well. I'm talking about goldfish, which can stretch to 12 inches or so. A variety of baits will work for these species, including dough-balls, worms, and corn; some have even reported success with pieces of half-baked (an appropriate description) macaroni.

Bullheads and sunfish are the next most willing biters. They tend to be on the diminutive side and are often located close to shore, whereas the bullheads tend to stay a bit deeper near the bottom—although in spring it's not unusual to catch one while dunking for sunfish. Worms are king here, and doughballs take honorable mention.

Yes, there is a decent population of largemouths in here, but they tend to be skittish, undoubtedly due to the onslaught of traffic, angler and nonangler alike. Best approaches are to use slightly larger, intact live worms here; if you can get your hands on some fathead minnows, those are worth a try also. Even when you do hook up, don't expect the next state record . . . although some fish of up to 14 inches or so are caught here now and again.

The park is in Jersey City alongside the Hackensack River. Parking is easiest in the lot between Duncan Avenue and Lake View Drive; the small pond is between Lake View Drive and Tennis Court Drive.

West Hudson County Park Pond

A summer evening here reminds me of the turn of the century—the 19th to the 20th century, that is. This is a pleasant park comprising some 10 acres or so, with the pond a featured attraction in the middle. You'll be joined by a number of people out enjoying the warm weather, some pushing strollers; the occasional kid dunking worms; bicyclists ped-aling along the paths. It all makes for an unusually pleasant setting. The water itself has plenty of insect life typical of ponds in the region, and lots of painted turtles to keep chil-dren both young and old delighted.

The water quality isn't exactly pristine, which means that outside of the springtime trout stocking (yes; use garden worms, mealworms, spinners, PowerBait, and the like during the early-spring stocking period), look primarily for hardy fish species that can take an environmental licking. Casual anglers will spend much of their time catching fair-to-middlin' sunfish on worms, while those with more patience may hook into a small largemouth bass or two.

Two species worth trying to reach are carp and catfish, both of which reach respectable proportions here. Try for the latter with as smelly a bait as you can muster and concentrate on low-light times. Carp seekers are advised to use a multiple arsenal of rods and reels baited with fruit- and/or dough-based offerings, in order to concentrate the fish's attention where you have your baited hooks.

The park may be reached from Schuyler Road in Harrison, near Newark. Turn onto Schuyler from Harrison Avenue, and turn west from Schuyler into the park after about 0.5 mile; there's plenty of parking available right next to the pond.

Woodcliff Lake

This is a 15-acre lake, making it the largest public lake within the county. It's also the central feature of North Hudson County Park, perched atop the Palisades and representing the highest point in Hudson County. It receives more attention from the state Division of Fish and Wildlife than many other water bodies, as it is stocked with, and continues to offer up, a nice variety of fish. Starting in spring, a number of trout are placed here both pre- and in-season. At about the same time, the sunfish and perch start to show more interest in taking your bait, while the modest yet willing largemouth bass will also take a carefully offered real or plastic worm, and sometimes grab that spinner meant for trout.

Channel catfish and their smaller cousins brown bullheads lurk within the depths as well, and people impaling chicken livers and tossing them to the bottom will be rewarded for their efforts. Finally, carp numbers are high here; anybody wanting to feel some real strength pulling on their line can bump up their tackle power level and try some corn or dough baits. The angling for all but the trout continues through summer and fall, and those with the itch come winter can try for trout again, as the state includes Woodcliff Lake in its winter trout-stocking program.

Angling is limited to the walkway surrounding the pond. Some places that might be worth extra effort include the fountains (when they're on), as these help to oxygenate the nearby water and can help to disguise anything that looks unnatural about your bait. The park is located at the north end of North Bergen, close to the Bergen County border, and is surrounded by 79th Street, Bergenline Avenue, Woodcliff Avenue, and J. F. Kennedy Boulevard East.

Morris County

Budd Lake

Budd Lake is a funny place. There are plenty of fish here, yet it's a rare day that you'll see more than a handful of anglers trying their luck. One reason is the lack of public launch facilities, although there is a private one that's not too expensive. The human-made lake is fairly shallow—about 6 feet over much of its expanse, with some deeper areas going down 9 to 12 feet not too far from the highway.

There's an impressive variety of fish here. Northern pike are the greatest attraction, and most of these toothy esocids are caught through the wintertime ice. Good pieces of equipment to keep handy for such an enterprise, in addition to your standard complement of hard-water tackle, include an auger (power is better; at the very least make sure the blades are as sharp as you can get them) and a sturdy gaff for lipping any pike that come in.

The relatively uniform weedy and shallow bottom is an important consideration in seeking pike; these conditions tend to distribute them fairly evenly. Your chances of success will therefore be good throughout the lake, but note that most of the regular ice anglers congregate along the western shore a few hundred yards from the nearby marina, near "The Castle" and easily accessed via Route 46.

Come spring, both largemouth and smallmouth bass lurk in the weedy areas, although the latter can be found in the deeper spots more readily as the weather warms. The chain pickerel is the other predominantly sought species here, and there are enough panfish, catfish, and suckers to keep any live-bait enthusiast happy.

Live herring and shiners are the ticket for the northern pike, although a slowly worked, oversized spinner or spoon can nail them occasionally. Largemouths and pickerel also go for the live fare but can be enticed by rattling crankbaits in spring and slow-rolled spinnerbaits and gently retrieved crankbaits in summer; the largemouths can also be found dwelling by the docks near Sand Shore Road. Use earthworms and crawlers for the panfish and catfish populations.

The intermediate or better angler will have the edge here because the lake is so fertile, with an abundant forage base. Shore anglers can make a fair showing for themselves, but using a boat will increase your score measurably. The bushy, *A nice New Jersey largemouth.*

swampy area opposite from the highway is a good place to work your baits slowly, carefully, and thoroughly.

Take Interstate 80 into Morris County, and get off the highway at Exit 26. Get onto Route 46 west. Head toward the towns of Mount Olive and Budd Lake; look for the large body of water on the right. If you'll be shore angling, you can simply park on the shoulder of the highway and walk to the water's edge (check for "no parking" areas). If you plan on boating, continue driving past the water, and make your first right onto Manor House Road to access the marina, where you can launch for a fee.

Lake Ames

Small and unassuming, this is a great place for some easy fishing on the way to or from work. It's even worth a trip in its own right for a family fishing or picnic excursion.

Weighing in at a mere 16 acres, it can be worked thoroughly in a morning or afternoon of effort, which is likely to pay off with satisfying benefits. Unlike many of the other waters covered in this volume, it isn't part of the state's trout-stocking program, which in many ways can work to an angler's advantage. The lake remains open to fishing during the three-week period prior to the trout season opener, and crowds are smaller in April and May. There are no boat-launching capabilities; in fact, there are large boulders blocking the entryway, allowing pedestrian but not vehicular ingress.

If you plan on fishing more than the picnic area, waders are practically a must, as there is plenty of wetland, uneven terrain, and mud surrounding the water. Be very careful with your footing; it was at this water that I nearly drowned in mud. One step I was on good terra firma, and the next I found myself chest-deep in muck.

Pickerel are likely to be your primary victims here, and they will go for a wide variety of offerings. Fly casters can do well; there are plenty of areas that allow for unimpeded back-casts. One area that you might be tempted, but ill advised, to overlook is the junction of the water's main body with the inlet stream on the pond's northwest corner. Many a hapless pickerel has succumbed to my bait at this spot.

Bass anglers make a reasonable showing for themselves here as well, with most of the catches in late spring and early fall responding to soft plastics, small spinnerbaits, and top-water offerings that are carefully presented. Panfish? For sure; sunfish and perch lead the charge in this category, and those with the drive and patience can hook into the occasional cat-fish and carp.

Take Interstate 80 to the exit intersecting Route 513, and follow that road north a few miles to Rockaway. Turn left onto Snake Hill Road, then turn right into the Lake Ames parking area.

Lake Hopatcong

This, the largest lake in the state of New Jersey, defies adequate description in a book this size. It has enough acreage, variety, and activity that volumes would be necessary to do it full justice. Here are some pointers that can, however, help you begin the process of unlocking the water's many secrets.

First, try to gain ac-cess to boating. There are various commercial launch sites and marinas, and at least one facility

Professional bass angler Pete Gluszek shows us how it's done, during a tournament on Lake Hopatcong.

(Dow's Boat Rental) can hook you up inexpensively for the day by hiring out small craft. If you're restricted to shore, you can either request permission to fish from one of the commercial enterprise's docks, or take your chances with one of the many private homes and docks surrounding the lake. In addition, there are a couple of public-access areas that are worth trying. One is the Windlass Restaurant (45 Nolans Point Park Road in the township of Lake Hopatcong; 973-663-3190); they open their property to ice fishermen in winter and may do so during the open-water months as well. Another is the Brady Road Bridge, if you can find nearby parking.

The action begins in earnest in April when the trout season opens, as the lake is stocked liberally by both the New Jersey Division of Fish and Wildlife and the Lake Hopatcong Knee Deep Club. Shore anglers do well with a variety of natural baits and small in-line spinners, while those in boats often troll any of a variety of lures, at different depths, to increase their catch rate.

At the same time, the pickerel, walleye, and muskellunge fisheries are hitting their stride in April and early May. Dock anglers cast diving crankbaits and depth-plumbing jigs for walleye after dark, while pickerel anglers explore the many weed beds all year.

By mid-April, the bass anglers are out in force; there's hardly a weekend between now and Labor Day that doesn't see at least one bass tournament on the lake. Largemouth and smallmouth bass are both present, and adhere to any of four primary patterns: docks, rock piles, weeds, and land points. A huge variety of lures and baits will land these freshwater staples; among the most popular are diving and surface plugs, soft stickbaits, plastic worms, and jig-and-pig (or jigs with other trailers) variants.

Lake Hopatcong is also home to one of the state's best hybrid striped bass fisheries. These "rockets" (as they are popularly known) are most active in early springtime, and can be found in the shallower areas like the Brady Bridge.

Freelining live herring is the key for these memorable battlers, although surface plugs often give a good account for themselves, and many like to go deeper with slip bobbers. As the season and water heat up into summertime, the fish will start moving into deeper waters.

The bass activity stays in high gear throughout spring and summer and well into autumn. By summertime, another species becomes an increasingly popular target: catfish. Channel cats lead the pride, with different species of bullheads filling out the menu. They often gravitate toward rocky structure—rock piles, ledges, and similar forms; occasionally a muddy bottom yields the odd catch as well. Nighttime angling is popular for these fighters, which can grow to upward of 30 pounds. Favorite baits are mullet, herring, and bluegill. A popular rig involves hooking a sunfish, placing some weight about 2 feet above it, then adding another hooked sunfish to that.

Walleyes and other cool-water species (holdover trout, muskellunge) continue to bite but tend to be caught from deeper waters at this time of year. Live bait (herring and shiners; larger specimens for the muskies), deepdiving plugs, and jigs are popular for these fish. A good sonar unit

Hybrid striped bass, called "rockets" by many, can be fearsome and downright crazy fighters. Knee Deep Club representative Tim Clancy shows us how big they can be.

to locate schools of baitfish can be of significant benefit. As autumn comes into prominence, the fish behave more like they did in spring, and angling patterns are best adjusted accordingly.

Those who prefer simpler angling can enjoy the many panfish varieties here, including bluegills, sunfish, crappie, perch, and rock bass. Some of the crappie in particular can be surprisingly chunky and are often caught while bass angling. Boat and shore/dock anglers do equally well on many of these varieties.

A couple of other points are worth bringing up. Lake Hopatcong is very popular among ice fishermen; the two primary species caught are chain pickerel and yellow perch. Also, there's a fine muskie fishery just after ice-out. Although this time period—around the month of March—is typically not very popular among freshwater anglers (and the lake is off-limits to fishing during the weeks prior to the opening of trout season), a few die-hard bass anglers have reported some of the best muskellunge fishing of the year at this time.

Where to start? Lake Hopatcong's sheer volume can make the place intimidating to anybody arriving here for the first time, and it's impossible—indeed, almost foolhardy—to attempt fishing the whole thing in a single day. It can be useful to think of the lake as a conglomerate of smaller bodies of water. Here are a few of them that can get you going.

The Great Cove is a popular spot; it's located along the eastern aspect of the lake adjacent to Nolan's Point. A simple way to get started here is to get to Dow's Boat Rental, located along the inner, northern part of the cove (along, appropriately enough, Nolan's Point Road in the town of Espanong). Sizable weed beds in this vicinity attract plenty of pickerel and bass, and other species often wander in as well. Shallow trolling can be effective, and those preferring to cast score on a variety of live and artificial baits.

Somewhat north of the Great Cove is Brady Bridge, so named because Brady Road traverses that narrow section of the lake there, also in Espanong. It's especially popular in spring, and popular catches include striped bass hybrids, walleyes, and bass. Herring almost always work well, and stickbaits with little to no intrinsic action can also be productive.

Another popular section is the area west of Raccoon Island, very close to where Chincopee Road in Woodport comes to the lake's edge. Depths here range from about 10 to 30 feet, and it's a proven spot for trout and hybrid striped bass. Byram Cove, southwest of the island, and Henderson Bay directly northwest can be fished with downriggers using artificial baits, while others do well drifting live herring. The inner sections of Henderson Cove are shallower and weedier and can provide good action for chain pickerel and largemouth bass, with a sprinkling of crappie tossed in.

Moving farther south along that western aspect of the lake, you'll encounter the irregularly shaped cove called River Styx. Mostly shallow and weedy, this a nice spot for more largemouth bass and pickerel, particularly in spring and summer. Those specializing in channel catfish have also reported good activity in the deeper sections of this region, closer to the main lake.

An excellent source of more information on this great fishery is through the Knee Deep Club, which is directly responsible for many of the great fishing opportunities here; its Web site is www.kneedeepclub.org.

Lake Musconetcong

Of all the public waters you might fish in New Jersey, Lake Musconetcong could be the most enigmatic. You're unlikely to see the legions of boaters, water-skiers, anglers, and miscellaneous marine recreationalists here that the other waters get; nor does it receive any of the publicity. There are reasons for this relatively light usage. The lake is unusually shallow—with a uniform depth of 5 to 6 feet—providing for plenty of weeds and lily pads, which is heaven for the lake's pickerel and largemouth bass population.

In early spring, the Division of Fish and Wildlife stocks the place with trout, accounting for a good number of anglers seeking these perky salmonids as well as panfish, using primarily live bait—although those who can find some open water in which to cast can score with in-line spinners. By late May, however, the lake comes into its own as a bass and pickerel fishery.

Lure selection should include plenty of weedless offerings, like a weighted or unweighted Texas-rigged worm; two good colors are red shad and pumpkinseed. Another good choice is any of the wacky worm styles of plastic worm rigging. (In fact, Jersey Riggs inventor Jeff Cammerino used this very same body of water as his research laboratory when he developed his revolutionary plastic worms.)

Other productive baits include soft plastic jerkbaits and single-hook spoons with weedguard. Frog and rat lures with a trailer hook in place, and the new toad lures, are effective when dragged over the surface growth. Other lures such as spinnerbaits and crankbaits also work where they can be

Will it be a sunfish, catfish, pickerel, bass, or trout? This young boy will soon find out.

cast, but be prepared to clean stuff off them after nearly every retrieve.

Alternatively, rig a small (3- to 5-inch) shiner or herring on a medium hook with a bobber about 12 to 15 inches in front of it, cast it out, and wait for the bobber to dive under the water. Scaled-down natural baits like worms and fathead minnows will attract some of the other species that inhabit this water, including catfish, perch, sunfish, and crappie.

If you don't have a small boat, you can rent one from the resident tackle store on the lake, Bait and Boat, which can also help with bait and tackle needs. The store is also open in winter; this lake happens to be one of the premier ice-fishing locations in the state.

Lake Musconetcong in Netcong is easily accessed from Interstate 80. At Exit 27, head toward Route 206 north. At the circle, keep following signs for 206 north. At the first traffic light, turn right, then turn left into the parking and launch area for the lake.

Mount Hope Pond

This 18-acre water is located in the town of Rockaway along Mount Hope Road, and is definitely worth a stopover anytime from April through September. One of the state's typical bass-and-panfish ponds, it's also stocked with trout. Most of the shoreline is wooded, with intermittent pathways providing easy access to the water; a beach and swimming area are located on the west side.

Waders will give you an advantage over anglers without them, as you'll be able to reach more water. In April and May, trout will respond to typical hatchery-imitating morsels dangled under a bobber, or attack a Mepps or Blue Fox spinner with gusto. Bait anglers will do well to keep the hook size from getting too small unless they don't mind continually reeling in bluegills, sunfish, or perch. Deeper water, to 12 feet, is easily reached all around the pond (except from the beach), providing trout activity throughout.

Springtime bass seekers will find plenty of specimens in the 1- to 2-pound range chasing small single-bladed spinner-baits or jointed crankbaits; interest shifts to small plastics (4-inch worms in muted colors or 3-inch stickbaits) by June and into summer. There's plenty of cover and structure and cover to probe for the resident largemouths. Good starting points include the tangle of laydowns in the northwest corner, the weed lines along the southwest area (especially in spring), and near the many rocks along the southern shore, opposite Mount Hope Road.

Catfishermen can find a respectable population of channel cats and bullheads, taking their share from popular bait varieties including chicken livers and large earthworms. The deepest water in the pond is most easily accessed from the Mount Hope Road side, so come in from that side, set up your gear, have a seat, and relax.

The pond is easily reached. Take Interstate 80 to Exit 35 and follow Mount Hope Road north a few miles. Look for the pond on the left; there are plenty of places to pull your vehicle over. There is also parking near the beach area.

Passaic County

Barbours Pond

In many ways, this is another underutilized water, located in Garrett Mountain Reservation in West Paterson. From April through September, this pond offers perfectly fine fishing for bluegill and pumpkinseed sunfish, with some yellow perch and crappie tossed in. They'll take a variety of offerings, with live bait like garden worms and mealworms leading the charge.

The largemouth bass population is well worth the effort. Small specimens will occasionally surprise the sunfish angler, but a more directed effort is required to land these surly fellows on a regular basis. Most bass run up to about 1.5 pounds, but there have been reports of individuals up to 6 pounds. Soft plastics are the key in most cases; topwater poppers and crankbaits also produce during low-light periods. Anglers have reported catches from virtually every section of the water except the far southern end.

This water has also been the beneficiary of channel catfish and carp infusions. Standard catfish offerings like stinkbaits, chicken livers, and large nightcrawlers will produce some respectable whiskered catches; switch over to smaller hooks with fruit-based dough baits—and somewhat heavier tackle—for carp.

The greatest draw that this spot has for anglers, however, is right at the beginning of the spring fishing season. The Division of Fish and Wildlife stocks the pond with trout before the season opens, and weekly for the next month. A variety of baits account for stringers of pre-dinner salmonids: real and imitation salmon eggs, corn kernels, PowerBait, garden worms, mealworms, and small spinners. Most of the action is concentrated by the rock formations up the small hill from Mountain Avenue. If you stop by this pond on a weekend in April or early May, and from about 5:30 to 7:00 PM on weekdays during this same period, you'll see folks taking advantage of the pond's bounty. Early morning, however, from about 5:30 to 8:00 AM on weekdays, you're likely to be the only one there. By June the crowds thin out even more.

Approach the area from Route 46, head north on Rifle Camp Road, go past the Great Notch Reservoir on the right, and bear right on Mountain Avenue. There's a small footbridge visible on the right, with parking available on both sides of Mountain Avenue. You can also turn right just past the footbridge, and follow the road into the reservation to a dedicated parking area.

Clinton Reservoir

This 423-acre Newark watershed reservoir is rich in structure. Examination of a topographic map reveals a veritable maze of points, drop-offs, islands (both aboveground and underwater), and coves. Depths range from a few feet up to 47 feet. Much of the bottom is covered with boulders (boaters, beware) interspersed with weeds, gravel, and mud.

Most early-season anglers target trout, which are amply stocked here both pre- and in-season, and the launch area (from which the stocking occurs) is an excellent place to try. In addition to worms, salmon eggs, and spinners, small fathead minnows will strike gold. Those who get out in the water will find that trolling takes a number of salmonids as well, including some of the larger holdover specimens. Likely spots are the deeper-water sections, particularly in the southeastern area near the dam, especially as the weather heats up in summer.

By late spring, many anglers look for pickerel, finding them in a fair variety of habitat on the reservoir, particularly in weedy areas near rock formations, coves, and points. Shallow-running crankbaits, spinnerbaits, and various topwater offerings, along with shiners and herring in the 2- to 5-inch size range, account for many of the pickerel hooked.

Bass hunters will be able to occupy their time fruitfully as well, as both largemouth and smallmouth bass can be found here. Bronzeback stockings began in the summer of 1992 with both fingerling and breeders, and anglers can attest to the success of these efforts. Seek them in the deeper waters that have rocky cover; crayfish (live and imitation) on your hook should serve well. Other offerings that can produce are jigs and tube lures.

Finding the largemouths can sometimes be a mite tricky. Much of the habitat where you'd typically search for them seems to be dominated by chain pickerel, especially in the shallower weedy areas. If you concentrate on the many mid-depth drop-offs, you'll probably be able to entice some of them with spinners, spinnerbaits, jigs (with or without trailers), and Texas- or wacky-rigged plastic worms.

Rounding out the menu are catfish and panfish (sunfish, perch, and crappie). The abundant sunfish population in particular makes for good kids' fishing, and can bolster your own ego if the larger gamefish don't feel like playing that day.

Access is simple. Follow Route 23 in Passaic County to Clinton, and go north on Clinton Road, which closely follows the reservoir's shoreline. Boat access is located about 1.5 miles farther. Shore fisherman can pull over at any likely-looking area and try their luck at the water's edge.

The NWCDC

There are four large bodies of water operated under the auspices of the Newark Watershed Conservation and Development Corporation (NWCDC)—Echo Lake, Oak Ridge Reservoir, Clinton Reservoir, and Canistear Reservoir. The 35,000-acre watershed area was opened in 1970 by the city of Newark for recreational and educational purposes. The NWCDC was created in 1974, to act on the recommendations of a 1972 Rutgers University study. This study indicated that although a large part of the property should not be developed, some of it could be without affecting the city's water supply or the area's ecology. The NWCDC manages and plans these activities.

Access is open to the public through a permit system, with appropriate fees. For more information on rules governing area usage, contact the NWCDC at 973-697-2850.

Echo Lake

This is the southernmost of the four Newark watershed lakes open to public use, located near West Milford in Passaic County. It totals about 300 acres, and it's shaped roughly like a rectangle with one of the long sides pinched in a bit. It doesn't have the same variety of bottom contours that some of the other NWCDC waters have, but there's plenty to keep the fish happy. It's generally bowl-like, with depth changes occurring in a reasonably predictable manner. Maximum depths reach 32 feet.

There are plenty of locations where you can find large-mouth bass, starting with the long line of riprap extending along the shore to the right of the launch area. Good bets include small to midsized soft jerkbaits, plastic worms, and large popping bugs. These latter can be cast with fly gear, ultralight spinning gear, or medium spinning gear with some additional weight (bobber or casting bubble).

Farther along the shoreline past the rocks, the weedy growth provides excellent bass cover. It can be worked successfully with a variety of lures: worms and jerkbaits again, Zara Spooks and Puppies, small crayfish-imitating crankbaits, and of course live bait.

Pickerel can be caught in these areas as well, but many anglers find them to be more numerous on the opposite side of the lake. Although they will take a well-presented artificial, live bait seems to run more to their taste, especially herring between 3 and 5 inches.

And, of course, muskellunge. First stocked here in 1991, many of these magnificent fish reach respectable proportions.

The chain pickerel is as native to New Jersey as you can get. Here the author admires a respectable "pick" from one of the Newark Watershed reservoirs.

Some suggested places to start are the shallower areas near the southern part of the lake, and the swampy area near the northern part. Like bass, muskies apparently relate to structure, but not necessarily cover. Keep an eye out for changes in bottom contour, shoreline configuration, and the like. Even though Echo Lake has few overt features in this category, there are a number of smaller, subtler ones that won't show up on the contour maps. And when you find baitfish congregated in such a spot, it's well worth probing carefully.

I wouldn't be doing justice to this lake if I didn't mention the panfishing potential. Some of the biggest bluegills and yellow perch I've seen have been caught here, and bullhead catfish are present in excellent numbers as well.

The lake is easily reached off Route 23 in Passaic County. Follow Echo Lake Road north from the highway; a sign for the launch area and put-in point will soon be to your left.

Green Turtle Pond

More than one person has named this pretty spot in the northern part of the county, located within the Wanaque Wildlife Management Area, as their home water, and these are people who live much closer to other fishing spots. Among its primary attractions are relatively pristine surroundings, ease of launching a small boat, a variety of structure attractive to fish, and the willingness of the local bass population to accept your offerings.

Trout anglers are advised to try other locations—this water isn't a stop on the stocking truck's route. Pickerel and bass action begins in earnest during mid- to late April, with rattling crankbaits and diving Rapala-style cranks covering water effectively. As the underwater growth thickens, weed-resistant baits come into their own, including toad lures, plastic worms, single-hook spoons, and small spinnerbaits. A good weed bed at which to start your efforts is the cove in the extreme southwest corner, to the left of the boat-launch area. Shoreline cover is plentiful, and those who work the shallows (to about 10 feet deep) should be rewarded.

Other species of interest include sunfish and perch (both white and yellow), and catfish—although reports on the catfish action here have been less than impressive; those who persevere in the deeper areas (the center of water, which goes to about 20 feet) are likely to have greater success.

Sandwiched in between Greenwood Lake and Monksville Reservoir, the water can be reached from Awosting Road, off Greenwood Lake Turnpike (Route 511) in Awosting. The access route is typically in poor repair, so be wary driving in and out. The 40-acre water favors those who have hauled in a small car-top vehicle—johnboat, rowboat, or canoe—to cover more water.

Greenwood Lake

The complexity and size of this lake, which straddles the New Jersey (Passaic County) and New York (Orange County) border, approach those of Lake Hopatcong, with which Greenwood shares many features.

The water, like many in the region, is very fertile and often experiences summertime algal blooms. The southern half of the lake has a predominantly muddy, silted bottom, and the remainder is characterized by boulders, rocks, sand, and gravel. The lake covers more than 1,900 surface acres, with depths ranging down to 50 feet covering plenty of submerged points and underwater islands, and hosts a large variety of year-round angling opportunities. With the exception of Brown's Point Park in Browns, the lake's perimeter is privately held. Access is, however, available through many of the commercial establishments and marinas dotting the lake's edge. It's a very popular site for local and regional bass-fishing tournaments, organized by groups from New Jersey, New York, and Pennsylvania.

In fact, Greenwood Lake is considered by some to be the finest bass-fishing water in our state, due to the great variety and abundance of bass-attracting structure and habitat: docks, weed beds, rock piles, and more. As in most lakes of this size and type, anglers target the weed beds and other relatively shallow areas with surface or fast-moving lures in the early morning and evening. As the heat of the day increases and the sun ascends, they tend to downsize and slow down their baits, offering them in deeper-water structures or around boat docks.

Although largemouth and smallmouth bass are both present, the former are more numerous, with specimens up to 6 and 7 pounds caught every year. The smallmouths can be respectable as well, going as high as 5 pounds. Early-spring anglers concentrate on the areas that are at least moderately deep, using fast-running lures like rattling crankbaits, and suspending jerkbaits. As the weather warms and the bass move shallow, experienced fishermen follow them into weedy and gravelly areas, slowing down their offerings of plastic worms, wacky-rigged Senkos, and other soft plastics.

A good area to try is the region surrounding Fox Island, located in the southern half of the lake. The channel directly west of it has good numbers of stumps and weeds; another field of weeds north of the elongated landmass is productive, and the nearby shallow bedding areas can be good spring through autumn. Don't restrict your largemouth hunting to this region, though—there are plenty of others.

Given a choice between deep rocks and shallow weeds, smallmouths invariably opt for the former, and you'll find plenty in the New York portion. If you can find spots that offer these with some underwater vegetation as well, work them that much more carefully.

Another big-game fishing attraction is the muskellunge. The opportunities for these large and ferocious-looking fighters keep getting better, with sizes of 45 inches and larger becoming more and more commonplace. Most are caught during the cooler open-water months (March, April, October, November) on large baits 6 to 10 inches long tied to heavy tackle; two favorite techniques are casting and trolling in and around docks as well as through weed beds.

Greenwood Lake is one of the premier locations in our state to hunt for the amazing muskellunge.

Walleye have come on strong here in recent years as well. With specimens up to about 7 pounds, they can usually be found during the cooler months and/or at night in the shallows. During summer, anglers find them in deeper water just above and within the upper portion of the thermocline (about 20 feet deep in this large lake).

Pickerel, perch, catfish, and sunfish are targeted here, too. Pickerel are often found in or near weeds, and can normally be caught with bass lures. Other fish varieties are well distributed and can usually be enticed with garden worms or nightcrawlers, whether fishing from boat, dock, or shore.

As a boundary water, Greenwood Lake has unique regulations, although many of these rules are quite similar to those governing the rest of New Jersey's waters. Either a New Jersey or New York license is legal when fishing anywhere on the lake itself (from a boat or on the ice); if you're fishing from shore, however, you must have a license legal for the soil on which you're standing. For the specifics of seasons and size/creel limits, consult the current freshwater fishing issue of the *New Jersey Fish and Wildlife Digest*.

Although Brown's Point is open to the public, it does not allow for boat launching. If you wish to do so, you must have an in with one of the private residences—or you can use one of the many commercial establishments. A good source for locating these is www.greenwoodlakenews.com/business/entertainment.html.

Monksville Reservoir

This reservoir, part of Passaic County's Wanaque River system, was impounded in the 1980s, with 505 acres of surface water in a rough horseshoe shape.

With an average depth of 43 feet and a maximum depth of 85, this reservoir (located in Ringwood and Hewitt) has a host of fish species lurking beneath its usually placid waters. Facilities include two boat-launch ramps and parking areas, all in excellent condition, and an access point designed specifically for the bank fisherman, with its own parking area.

One of the most popular gamefish is the largemouth bass, with representatives well distributed over the various structural features including numerous drop-offs, humps, points, coves, weed beds, and flooded timber. Typical bass offerings, including plastic worms, spinnerbaits, crankbaits, and of course the always popular live baits, will produce here. Low-light periods near dawn and dusk often see good topwater action.

Smallmouth bass have also been established within the watery depths, providing one of the premier smallmouth fisheries in New Jersey. Rocky structure, of which there is plenty, often attracts them. Chain pickerel are plentiful and can usually be enticed by shiners or herring, although they're also taken by typical bass lures. Their larger cousins the muskellunge enjoy healthy population levels; in fact, the state-record muskellunge was taken through the ice at Monksville in 1997.

The panfisherman can have a field day here. Most of the species available in New Jersey can be caught: bluegill, pumpkinseed, and redbreast sunfish; white and yellow perch; rock bass; and crappie. There is an area near Beech Road, at

Bob Neals holds the muskellunege that earned him the state record: a 42-pound, 13-ounce monster caught from Monskville Reservoir.

the northeast corner of the impoundment, designed especially for bank fishermen, who usually have good luck with sunnies there. Perch tend to be found somewhat deeper, and crappie may be sought in the brushy sections of the reservoir's northeast section.

Trout are stocked liberally, and the hospitable habitat allows some of them to hold over and grow—many of them to respectable sizes. Try suspending live bait in some of the deeper water toward the dam, and trolling some of the deeper sections.

Monksville may be the flagship of the state's recently developed walleye program, as this great fish showed signs of successful adaptation to the lake soon after it was introduced, in the early 1990s. Mid- to late autumn usually finds a number of hopefuls plying the shoreline near the launch ramps with live and artificial offerings. During the warmer months, it's almost mandatory to be plumbing the deeper waters for these toothy gamefish.

Most of the species described here are also taken readily through the ice by wintertime hard-water anglers.

Location and access are easy. Follow Ringwood Avenue (Route 511) north in Passaic County. It becomes Greenwood Lake Turnpike; keep following it. Go past the Wanaque Reservoir on the left, and watch out for the dam on the left. You will soon see the first launch and parking area access driveway on your left. If you pass this, and continue on, the road soon goes right over the reservoir. Just before that, you can either peel off to the left for the second boat launch and parking area, or peel off to the right onto Beech Road for the bank-fishing parking area. (Bank fishing is available at any of the parking areas.)

Oak Ridge Reservoir

This reservoir, part of the Newark Watershed Conservation and Development Corporation holdings in the northern part of the state, comprises 482 surface acres in an amorphous, elongated, slightly curved configuration. Examination of a topographic map shows a richness in bottom contour lines, with holes as deep as 46 feet as well as sunken islands. Much of the shoreline area hosts attractive drop-offs, accompanied in large part by subsurface growth.

If you like bass, both smallmouth and largemouth, then a visit or two here is well worth your while. The smallmouth action in particular is considered outstanding among New Jersey's waters. Much of the reservoir's bottom is covered with rocks, and fish-holding weed patches of various sizes are scattered about.

Two main forage sources in this reservoir are crayfish and small baitfish, so select your imitations accordingly. If the baitfish seem to be reasonably active (you will often see them dimpling the surface, sometimes jumping right out), then a fast-moving minnow imitation can work; good choices include Rat-L-Traps and Rebel jointed minnow crankbaits. Good crayfish imitators are small crayfish-shaped crankbaits, and

Texas-rigged crayfish plastics with a little weight attached. Jig-and-pigs (or other trailers) are effective as well.

Those targeting the equally impressive largemouth population will score on those baits already mentioned, and will also likely have good luck with spinnerbaits, especially in brown and orange colors. If these seem to be a bit slow in drawing attention, real crayfish can be the ticket.

Shoreline drop-offs are excellent starters; one area in particular is along the east shore, past the area surrounding the launch. Much of the nearshore water drops off in depth fairly gradually, and bass are often found in these spots.

The ever-popular pickerel is the other primary larger gamefish to be found here. Members of the chainsides gang will be attracted primarily to whatever weedy areas you can locate. The water also harbors good populations of sunfish, yellow perch, and bullheads, all of which are happy more often than not to grab your worm; the former two will often chase down a small in-line spinner.

Drive along Route 23 until you get to the Oak Ridge area. Follow Reservoir Road off the highway, and within less than 100 yards look for the launch-area access to your right.

Sussex County

Canistear Reservoir

The only Newark watershed body outside Passaic County, this 350-acre reservoir is roughly rectangular and contains a respectable variety of fishing opportunities, focusing primarily on trout, bass, and pickerel. Like some of the other watershed bodies, Canistear is stocked yearly with trout, some of which manage to survive to good-sized proportions, often up to 4 pounds. Although many of the smaller stockies may be had from shore in early spring on the usual live and natural baits, most experienced trout seekers take to their boats to search out the big browns and rainbows via drifting or trolling.

To drift successfully, simply sink your bait to about 15 feet deep, align your boat with the breeze, and let Mother Nature take her course. In particular, I recommend the stretch of lake right in front of the boat ramp. Those who prefer to troll (electric motors only here) use either natural bait or an artificial such as a spoon or Rapala crankbait. Both drifting and trolling can be effective right through summer and autumn, especially on overcast days.

For bass action, you can take your pick between largemouths or smallmouths. The bigmouths tend to be somewhat more predictable and widespread, and therefore account for a larger proportion of the total bass catch than do the smallies. Start by targeting the weed beds, which are scattered over the reservoir. Dark plastic worms account for many bass, and topwaters—poppers, Spooks, floating crankbaits—also take their share, especially around the edges of these beds.

Deeper-water drop-offs often harbor fish when the weed beds don't. Good offerings to try include jigs, with and without trailers. Spinnerbaits, slow-rolled or hopped along these drop-offs, can also be worth investigating.

You may well pick up the occasional smallie while working the drop-offs with your spinnerbaits or jigs. Other, more targeted approaches include using tube lures, crayfish-imitating crankbaits, and live crayfish.

You're likely to connect with one or more pickerel while probing the weed beds, especially if you opt for live bait. To round out the Canistear Reservoir possibilities, there are, of course, plenty of panfish, with the yellow perch seeming to be most plentiful. Schools of them can be found in the middle reaches of the reservoir, and good choices for bait include worms and very small diving crankbaits. Sunfish populations are dominated by the small, colorful, and aggressive redbreast. They work the shorelines, ready to grab almost anything they can get their mouths around.

To reach this reservoir—located just west of Jefferson and West Milford in Passaic County—follow Route 23 to the

southern part of Sussex County, and take Canistear Road
north. Signs marking the launch area will soon be evident on
your left.

Cranberry Lake

Cranberry Lake weighs in at 179 acres and holds a soft spot in
my heart as a solid, all-around fishery. Despite many people's
claims that the fishing quality has deteriorated in recent years
(blame is put on a variety of factors, from the unlimited horsepower allowance to the use of septic tanks on surrounding
properties), you can go there virtually anytime with a reasonable expectation of a nice day of fishing.

In many respects Cranberry is reminiscent of Lake
Hopatcong, with fishing patterns centered on docks, rock
piles, and various weedy areas. Primary fishing targets are
largemouth bass and pickerel, but some determined anglers
seek the northern pike—admittedly on the unpredictable
side here, at times—that dwell within, thanks to the ongoing
stocking program.

Spring is the best time for northern activity, when you
can get away from those seeking the stocked trout.
Recommended locations are near the island and dam; spinners and spinnerbaits have produced well, as have some
surface lures. As the weather starts to warm, most bass
anglers find their success rate is maximized using smaller
baits and lures, preferably those with little intrinsic action,
given this spot's popularity. Small worms, Gitzits, tubes,
and jerkbaits account for many of the bass taken. Some
smallmouth bass come to hand, but largemouths dominate
the black bass niche.

The primary panfish seen here are bullheads and sunfish,
with yellow perch coming in with a strong showing as well;
miniature jigs and live-bait offerings turn many a piscine head
in these categories.

Wintertime ice anglers have discovered that the pickerel
and pike opportunities here are also worth investigating; well-

placed shiners and skillfully worked jigs have brought respectable numbers of these species, as well as yellow perch and the occasional bass sunfish, through the fishing hole.

Although there are limited shoreline angling opportunities, boating is the way to go here. This is especially true in light of the unlimited horsepower possibilities. The boat ramp is accessible via South Shore Road; turn right into the driveway soon after getting onto South Shore. Although maneuvering a boat trailer is a mite tricky here, and there is parking for only about half a dozen vehicles with trailers (overflow parking is available farther along South Shore Road), the ramp itself is in good condition, with a dock handy. South Shore Road, in turn, can be reached from Route 206 in Byram.

Hainesville Pond

This 37-acre, weed-infested pond has seen a rejuvenation of larger gamefish populations in recent years. For some time it was known primarily as a place where youngsters could dip a line for sunfish and bullheads, but the largemouth bass and chain pickerel have been thriving since the turn of the millennium.

Although trout have been stocked here in some years, they are not added on a regular basis; it behooves you to look into this before making the journey. Even if trout aren't available, however, early-season opportunities are plentiful for some of the other fish already mentioned. The trout angler is likely to see plenty of sunfish, a smattering of perch, and some pickerel and bass showing interest in those worms or spinners tossed into the April and May waters. Fly anglers can have plenty of fun tempting all of these fish with surface poppers, sized according to the species sought.

By June, the weed growth will be plentiful enough to mandate weedless baits; those using natural bait can get by using hooks with wire weedguards. Surface lures will still work but are best deployed early in the day and late at night.

Because there are no boat-launching facilities here, nor any obvious means to get a car-top vessel into the water, you'll be well served with a good pair of chest waders to reach as much water as possible. Another option worth investigating is a float tube.

Access to the water, located within the Hainesville Wildlife Management Area, is via Route 206 north of Sandyston; turn onto Shaytown Road, make a left onto Cemetery Road, and the pond will be on the right.

Jefferson Lake

This is a 50-acre lake, located in Byram and Lockwood near Allamuchy State Park. The first thing to keep in mind is that, while the water itself is public domain, access to the water is available only via the public launch facility that you'll encounter on arrival. The adjacent camp's land is private property, and the occupants are very serious about keeping it private.

This lake is best explored with a small car-top vessel. The water's small size makes it easy to paddle or oar about the entire periphery and interior (okay, use a trolling motor if you must), and it will enable easy avoidance of unnecessary turf battles. It's possible to work much of the surrounding shoreline on foot, but there are substantial obstacles that make it difficult if not prohibitive.

Largemouths here grow to be decent size in these often murky waters. It's common to see specimens up to 3 pounds, and there are reports of a respectable number of 4- and 5-pounders. They behave as most bass do and respond to the standard fare of offerings. Because visibility is often poor in these submerged haunts, take some precautions keep your offering visible while at the same time maintaining as natural a presentation as possible. This suggests brighter colors than normal, adding some extra action to those lures, or concentrating on baits that appeal to the fish's lateral line or hearing senses (spinnerbaits, crankbaits, and the like). Subtle plastics like worms and jerkbaits can work fine; just be sure that you've done something to its appearance (a splash of red or chartreuse) or action (some extra twitches that you might not ordinarily have tried) to help the prey notice it.

A good place to spend some time is the lily pad patch across from and slightly to the left of the launch area, close to camp property. Start with its periphery and work your way inward, always giving first priority to apparent edges. The cove directly to the pad field's left (if you are facing the camp) is quiet and unobtrusive, and has yielded more than one photo-worthy bucketmouth to a skillfully worked bait. And then the shore area on the other side of the pads is worth some casts as well, all the way around its bend.

If the water—and your boat's freeboard—are sufficiently low, try sneaking under the bridge to what my oldest son and I refer to as "pickerel cove," owing to the outstanding pickerel action we've seen there on more than one occasion.

Take Interstate 80 to Exit 25 (Stanhope-Newton). Follow Route 206 north to the second traffic light, and turn left onto Waterloo Road (look for a Shell station on the left corner, and the Byram Diner on the right). Follow the road in for approximately 0.5 mile; before you get to the bridge, look for the small parking and launch areas on the left. (Continuing on the bridge will bring you into the camp, which is private property.)

Lake Aeroflex

No discussion of northern New Jersey lakes would be complete without Lake Aeroflex. Reported to be one of the deepest glacial lakes in the state, it covers about 117 acres and goes as deep as 100-plus feet, with a 39-foot average. Although there are a variety of fish to be had here throughout the year, the two primary targets are largemouth bass and brown trout.

The combination of relatively easy access, good fishing conditions, surrounding scenic beauty (yes, even the adjacent airport), and small size can make for some crowded conditions, especially on the weekends. If weekday visits fit into your schedule, this is well advised.

Popular approaches to bass angling include a variety of lures: jigs with trailers, spinners and spinnerbaits, and paddle-tail plastic worms. There is virtually no artificial structure to home in on, and many of the successful anglers seek out the submerged weed lines. This has the benefit of also pin-pointing the chain pickerel that are present, many of which grow to impressive size (reportedly foraging on the rainbow trout that are stocked here regularly). Typical tribe members come in at between 1 and 2 pounds, with 3- to 5-pounders sur-prisingly commonplace.

The trout population is subject to attention as well, including regular stockings by the Division of Fish and Wildlife as well as additional brown trout planted by the Aeroflex Trout Club. This is truly a year-round fishery: During the open-water seasons, anglers catch their share of rainbow or brown trout, many of them with trolled, down-rigged baits (including naturals, spoons, and spinners).

To use this approach, boating is of course required, and only electric motors are allowed. Shoreline anglers never-theless have a good shot at some quality fish, if they con-centrate efforts to just before and after ice-out for trout, and during low-light times the rest of the year for bass. There are plenty of panfish here as well, especially bluegill, yellow perch, and crappie (often up to 15 inches, especially through the ice in winter).

And the late-breaking news for this water? Salmon. The New Jersey Division of Fish and Wildlife stocked this water, along with Wawayanda Lake, with landlocked salmon (a variety of Atlantic salmon) in May 2006, and this has the potential to turn into a very exciting fishery. Troutlike approaches will undoubtedly be a good starting point when the salmon get to be of fishable size; contact representatives of the division for more suggestions.

Access is no problem. Head toward Kittatinny State Park; get onto Limecrest Road (Route 669) and look for the entrance within another mile or two.

Ryker Lake

You can use a boat and motor (electric only) in this unassuming, 30-acre water—if you can get them in. You'll have to traverse a substantial length of overland terrain, perhaps a quarter mile, from the place you park your vehicle to the lake's shore.

Walk-in-only access, although sometimes inconvenient, does have a silver lining. It tends to keep the crowds thin, and the boating fleet way down. If you're going solo, you can portage in a canoe or opt for a float tube. Lack of heavy boating also serves to leave the aquatic plant life intact— another double-edged sword for anglers, for although it provides tons of excellent fish habitat, it's that much tougher to actually fish.

Starting in late spring, the first thing you'll notice is the extended expanse of lily pads, covering 10 percent or more of the lake's surface at its summer peak. These are amply supported by both the lack of boating traffic and the relative shallowness of the lake—it reaches a maximum depth of only about 8 feet.

The state manages this water primarily to maximize angling opportunities for largemouth bass, yellow perch, and sunfish, although there are worthwhile numbers of pickerel, bullheads, and crappie here as well. It has been designated as a Conservation Regulations water, meaning that only two bass—each at least 15 inches long—may be in possession during the season, and no more than 10 sunfish (at least 7 inches each) and 10 yellow perch.

Best attempts to target the bass and chain pickerel have centered on the pads, using weedless frogs and worms. Depending on your casting accuracy, a well-placed popper in one of the many pad openings will often cause a basement dweller to come crashing up to see what the commotion is all about. Just be sure to have a heavy or braided line so you can tear it—lure, line, fish—free. The panfish (sunfish, perch, and crappie) are best targeted with live bait, but a skillfully worked spinner and other small artificials can fit the bill just as handily.

To reach this lake, head over to Sussex County's Route 620 near the Morris County border, in Sparta, and turn onto Edison Road—look for the Sparta Mountain Wildlife Area sign. Once you're on Edison, immediately look to the right for some boulders blocking off a small dirt road. Park your car there and hoof on in.

Swartswood Lake

Often called Big Swartswood, to distinguish it from its diminutive neighbor Little Swartswood Lake (a worthy multispecies fishery, including largemouth bass, in its own right), this 494-acre water in Swartswood was until recently greatly underutilized. To be sure, there has been a constant stream of anglers over the years, but it has only been since the early years of the millennium that the lake has come into its own as a premier fishing spot.

The two primary species sought are largemouth bass and walleye. The latter—stocked here since the early 1990s—have been growing fat on the native herring and yellow perch populations, establishing Swartswood as perhaps the finest walleye destination in the state. There are plenty of deep-water spots to plumb (most of the lake is deeper than 10 feet), and in spring and part of summer a surprisingly large number of the goggle-eyed fish are caught on surface baits. During periods of elevated temperature and light, savvy fishermen use vertically presented jigs and natural baits, as well as deep-diving crankbaits, to hook the walleyes.

Largemouths are only half of the bass story here, though; plenty of smallmouth bass lurk as well. Both species follow their genetic imperatives. Look for the smallies near the plentiful rock piles and the largemouths in and around vegetative cover (including the often expansive lily pads) and docks. Worms will work on both; Senkos pro-

Walleye are doing quite well these days in a number of New Jersey waters, including Swartswood Lake.

duce for the bigmouths, while finesse worms account for plenty of bronzebacks.

Pickerel and rock bass are two by-species that you're likely to see when angling for bass. Others that can be worth a more targeted approach include channel catfish, yellow perch, trout, sunfish, bullheads, and crappie.

Although there are adequate places for shoreline angling, boaters will have the edge. Electric motors are the only legal powered propulsion, and the boat launch is in good shape. It can be reached by taking Route 521 (Hope–Blairstown Road) north from Interstate 80, turning right onto Route 94, and going about 11 miles to Anderson Hill Road. Turn left and make the first right to stay on Anderson Hill, then turn left onto Route 622. When you reach the intersection of Routes 519 and 619, turn left onto 619; look for the entrance to Swartswood State Park and the boat launch.

Warren County

Deer Park Pond

This 46-acre lake, located in the heart of Allamuchy State Park, is one of the older naturally occurring waters in northern New Jersey, and is in virtually untouched condition. The final 0.5-mile stretch of the access road is open to pedestrian and bicycle traffic only, resulting in a barricade that effectively keeps all motor vehicles, and insufficiently motivated anglers, out. Those who make the effort, however, are usually well rewarded. Bucketmouths appear most often in the 1- and 2-pound class, but a good number of specimens in the 3- to 5-pound range have been seen as well. And the pickerel action can be nonstop at times.

Starting in spring and lasting well into fall, nearly half of the lake is covered with lily pads. As such, good starting baits include weedless frogs and spoons worked over the pads' surfaces. Those who are handy with a fly rod or ultralight spinning gear can see excellent action by twitching a smallmouth-sized bass popper in between the pads. Underwater baits like soft plastic jerkbaits and spinnerbaits worked around the pad beds' edges and indentations will get the attention of some of the resident lunkers as well.

The water can be reached by taking Interstate 80 to Exit 19 in Allamuchy, following County Road 517 south for a couple of miles, and turning left onto the dirt Deer Park Road (look for Mattar's restaurant on the right). Follow the road in as far as you can.

Furnace Lake

This water is referred to by some as Oxford Furnace Lake, and by a few as "53 acres of bass heaven." But good bass action is actually only a part of the picture here, as this lake may be the premier multispecies fishery in its locale. The state stocks it with trout in March and April, and (depending on the year) again in autumn, providing year-round trout opportunities—including summer, thanks to the presence of a trout-tolerable thermocline with sufficient oxygen. In spring-time, many of these trout are caught by anglers trolling small lures behind their boats or using natural bait under bobbers. As the weather warms to summer, they can be found at levels about 12 feet deep, and when the water begins to cool in late September they start to roam about again.

The bass population is dominated by largemouths, with smallmouths coming in a respectable second. Most anglers concentrate on the lake's periphery, especially the more heavily weeded areas, throwing lures like light-colored plastic worms (rigged either wacky or Texas style), crankbaits, spin-nerbaits, and buzzbaits. Reports of impressive specimens originate from these waters, including at least one largemouth just shy of 9 pounds.

Perhaps the next most abundant fish here is the crappie, specifically black crappie. Any of a number of live and artifi-cial baits will serve. Popular entrants in the latter class include spinners, small jigs, and plastic grubs, and it isn't unusual to see individuals of this tribe in excess of a pound. Perch and sunfish will at times compete for these offerings as well.

In the pike family, the ever-present chain pickerel often makes its bid to grab your bait first, particularly if you're probing weedy areas for any of the bass. And this lake has been subject to muskellunge stocking as well, including both full-strains and tigers. Stocking of the former was attempted in the early 1990s—an effort that apparently stopped there—but the tiger program continued, providing a good chance to hook one of these starkly patterned fighters. Many of those that are caught turn up as by-catch for anglers targeting bass or pickerel. Those who are serious about targeting tigers have better success using good-sized live baitfish like shiners or herring.

The channel catfish population here is also the subject of many anglers' efforts. Individuals in double-digit poundage turn up fairly often, and usually fall to cut baitfish, worm balls,

Many people consider Furnace Pond to be one of the premier ice fishing locations in northern New Jersey. Here, a hopeful youngster waits patiently.

and cut livers (chicken liver is always a favorite). Finally, I'd be remiss if I failed to mention that many people consider Furnace one of the best ice-fishing spots around. It's common for anglers to pull up a variety of species on a given outing; leading the pack are pickerel, perch, trout, and crappie.

The lake is in Oxford. The main entryway, off Route 625, leads to a parking area and launch facility with dock; only electric motors may be used. Because Furnace is located within a park of sorts, it's worth checking with local authorities if you plan on trying your luck in the autumn or winter—it's subject to closure in favor of waterfowlers.

Merrill Creek Reservoir

At 650 acres, this is easily the largest lake in the county. It is a major attraction of the Merrill Creek Environmental Preserve and as such is subject to preserve authority. It's also a very scenic area; many visitors, anglers and otherwise, are fortunate enough to get a view of one or more of the bald eagles that make their home here. And it offers fishing on a different level.

Bankbound anglers can at times do okay for themselves, especially if they limit themselves to springtime fishing and/or targeting panfish, but if you're serious about getting decent numbers of sizes of fish here then a boat is virtually mandatory (although there is a recent story of a young girl who caught a 3-pound largemouth bass on a live shiner from the boat ramp). Start your trip here by understanding that it this a large, deep impoundment, with depths in excess of 200 feet, and an average of around 75 feet. The deepest areas are, as you would expect, near the dam.

The biggest stories—and fish—here are smallmouth bass and lake trout. It's not unusual to catch a limit of smallmouth here in the 3- to 4-pound range, especially in springtime. The largemouth action can be similarly good, though by the time June comes around it can be difficult to locate the fish. There are some substantial drop-offs and areas of submerged timber,

This pretty "bronzeback," as smallmouth bass are often referred to, is representative of the catches that often show up from Merrill Creek Reservoir as well as other waters in the state.

and these are good places to try. A depthfinder can make all the difference in your efforts, so don't leave it at home. Don't be afraid to try real depths of 30 and 40 feet for both species. They can respond either to live or artificial baits. If you use the latter, jigging or careful trolling (along the appropriate depth lines) can produce.

After Round Valley Reservoir, this is probably the premier lake trout opportunity in the state. Again, however, seeking these potential giants requires a substantial investment of equipment, time, and effort. Probing 70 feet, 80 feet, and deeper is standard practice to catch these big salmonids. The prevailing conditions create some impressive brown and rainbow trout as well. The state provides a liberal infusion of stocked specimens midseason, allowing shoreline fishermen a chance to get in on the action, and helping to replenish the holdover fishery. Note that, along with Round Valley, this is a Trophy Trout Lake with special regulations: Brown and rainbow trout may be creeled all year, but the daily limit is two, and each must be 15 inches or longer. Lake trout may be kept January 1 through September 15 and during December; only one may be kept, and it must be at least 20 inches.

There are some restrictions in force here unique to this preserve. All boats must be at least 12 feet long (except kayaks, 9 feet; inflatables, 10 feet). Electric motors only are allowed, although gas motors need not be removed and may be used in an emergency. All boaters must launch from the boat ramp, and nowhere else on the shoreline. The preserve and boat ramp are open from 6 AM to 8 PM, daylight permitting, and the ramp is open all year unless locked up from ice (no ice fishing is allowed). Others rules are posted at the facility and on www.merrillcreek.com.

Mountain Lake

Touching the eastern border of Jenny Jump State Forest in the town of Liberty, 122-acre Mountain Lake can provide a relaxing day of productive fishing for the casual and serious angler alike. It goes down to about 38 feet near its center, with more or less uniform-depth drop-offs around that center. The more pronounced depth changes tend to be along the western shore, north of the launch area, and on the eastern shoreline.

March through April, the state stocks an assortment of brook, brown, and rainbow trout. These are typically sought by the usual onslaught of early-season anglers lining the shores, using the commonplace but reliable garden worms, mealworms, salmon eggs, and spinners. Other fish that often respond to these morsels are chain pickerel, carp, sunfish, perch, crappie, and bullheads.

In summer, those who seek largemouth bass can find them along the drop-offs mentioned (jigging works well), as well as within the weedy areas in the northern and southern parts of the lake using weedless spoons and soft plastic lures. During the height of vegetative growth, a carefully worked plastic rat or frog can trigger some heart-stopping surface strikes. Trout can still be had during these months; try some live bait about 8 to 10 feet down.

Pickerel are another group of willing takers, cooperating pretty much year-round with both natural and artificial baits. And in the cooler months (March and April, then again from late September through November), try your hand at some of the tiger muskellunge, which can top the 28-inch mark here. Good lure choices are small to medium crankbaits, spinner-baits, and jerkbaits (the hard plastic kind, like a Suick, for the tigers) in the shallow to medium-depth areas.

Boats may be launched from the ramp located on the western shore. The lake can be reached from Mountain Lake Road (Route 617) just east of Jenny Jump State Forest.

White Lake

This lake's plain round appearance could, on casual inspection, lead you to believe that it's a featureless, perhaps sterile bowl of water, but nothing could be further from the truth. A closer look will show that it has a variety of sunken weeds, emergent vegetation, and steep drop-offs all along its perimeter. A few crumbling docks provide silent evidence of previous private ownership, as well as some fish structure.

The edges are characterized by marl flats, ranging from perhaps a few yards to 50 yards in width, which then give way to a center bottom that goes quickly to 30 feet (down to 65 feet in one spot). The lake offers 65 surface acres, and is fished most efficiently from a canoe or johnboat. Either a trolling motor or oars can be useful, and those who wish to work the shallow flats in search of sunfish and largemouth bass may actually be better off with oars or paddles, as a trolling motor on even a short shaft will get fouled in the crumbly bottom more often than you'd like.

Bass hunters trying these shallows will find that the light-colored substrate makes for unusually good sight fishing. Most of the specimens are small, but a few good-sized fish up to 5 pounds roam these shallow flats in search of an easy meal. The lack of depth seems to accentuate the disturbance of big or noisy lures, so go with smaller and subtler presentations like worms, soft jerkbaits, and wacky-rigged worms. The latter, particularly in gold colors, are especially well suited to this water.

Next, try the inside edge of the flats. The drop-off attracts a good number of gamefish, and falling lures like weighted worms and jigs can attract their attention. For this as well as other applications here, try using a clear monofilament line. Trolling a small-to-medium spoon or crankbait in the deeper central section can get the attention of the lake's bass or pickerel, particularly the latter.

Baitfishermen score very heavily on the outstanding sunfish and bluegill population, and turn up the occasional yellow perch, bullhead, and eel as well; trout are stocked in the middle of the spring stocking time.

The lake has ample parking and a launch area (albeit fairly primitive). You can locate White Lake on Route 521 in Warren County near mile marker 9, about 3 miles northeast of Blairstown.

7

NORTHERN NEW JERSEY RIVERS AND STREAMS

Bear Swamp Brook

This pretty flow typifies the Wild Trout Stream program in New Jersey. It runs clean and pristine through relatively untrammeled land and can provide a morning or afternoon of quiet introspection. Restrictions on fishing equipment, and realistic limitations on the size of the trout swimming within, tend to keep the crowds away, as does the limitation on vehicular traffic. All this works in favor of the stream's natural beauty.

Wild trout are the story here. *Wild* in this context is a bit misleading; these fish are not descendants of native trout that were indigenous to the region centuries ago. Rather, the water quality here is high enough that the introduced brook, rainbow, and brown trout have established self-sustaining populations. Typical representatives are small but very feisty and colorful.

Anglers are limited to artificial tackle in this and similar streams. This translates in reality to very diminutive flies and tiny spinners, although some intrepid experimenters have had success with miniature spoons or jigs. Flies should be in sizes 20 or so; dry patterns that have worked include Elk Hair Caddis, Tent Wing Caddis, Adams, and Royal Wulff. Subsurface flies can include Muddler Minnows, Hare's Ears, Scuds, and Zug Bugs.

Hip boots are best for your time here; chest waders are too much. Fly gear should be light (no more than, say, 4-weight), and spinning gear should be short and ultralight. Leave the net at home, but bring a pocket camera with some macro or zoom capability (and built-in flash)—these eye-popping little fish are very photogenic. This is quiet, relaxed fishing, so take time to look for wildlife and enjoy the surroundings.

Head toward northern Bergen County along Route 202. In Mahwah, locate the private road known locally as either Bear Swamp Road or Cannonball Road. Look for nearby parking and hoof in along the brook, which parallels the private road.

Big Flat Brook

No discussion of New Jersey trout streams would be complete without Big Flat Brook. Considered by many to be the state's best, it originates deep within High Point State Park and makes its way down to its final joining with the Delaware River. It also has the honor of being specifically mentioned in the 1938 classic of trout-angling literature, Ray Bergman's *Trout*.

There are many spots along its length that attract the spring-through-autumn angler, but a couple of areas maintain their productivity in winter as well. Cold-weather anglers can try the 4-mile fly-fishing-only stretch in Sussex County, which begins at the Route 206 bridge in Sandyston and meanders down to the Roy Bridge on Mountain Road (Walpack). Another stretch, the Blewett Tract, which extends for 0.5 mile from Three Bridges Road to a point upstream of the Big Flat Brook and Little Flat Brook junction, is also especially deserving of attention. Although this beat is restricted to fly fishing, anglers may still creel up to the daily limit of trout if they wish.

Try exploring the gravel roads that wander around and across Route 615, also known as Walpack–Flatbrook Road in Sandyston, near Route 206. Those with the time and some spirit of exploration can try any of the feeder tributaries that spill into the Flat Brook. Short rods in light weight are the key, owing to the brushy conditions surrounding much of the stream. This, as well as its popularity, also makes for a wary trout population. Mayflies in Blue-Winged Olive, Light Cahill, Sulphur, and March Brown patterns are good, as are a number of generic stonefly and caddis imitations.

Depending on the location, you might also encounter creek chubs, smallmouth bass, and grass pickerel. Look for the Flat-brook-Roy Wildlife Management Area on your map of Sussex County, as much of this stretch flows through this preserve.

Black River

Although this river is over 10 miles long, probably the most popular fishing area lies within the very scenic Hacklebarney State Park in Morris County (Washington and Chester). Access is easy due to the park's popularity among hikers, bird-watchers, and anglers, and the water itself is simple enough to fish, with a good variety of shallow runs and riffles interspersed with deeper pools holding some trout—many with some impressive proportions. The park can be reached by taking Route 206 to Chester, and from there following Route 24/513 west for a mile to State Park Road for 2 miles. Turn right onto Hacklebarney Road and travel 0.5 mile; the entrance is on the left.

As the river makes its way farther south, access can get tougher and the habitat begins to morph over to slower waters more appropriate to smallmouths, which you will start to find here in more frequency as you head toward the Raritan River's North Branch. Bait anglers will also score on some chubs and suckers as incidental catches.

Delaware River (Northern Sections)

"The Big D" is one of the major rivers in the Northeast, and has enough angling opportunities year-round to keep almost any weekend angler occupied for many years. The most popular species are striped bass, shad, smallmouth bass, muskellunge, and walleye, but those targeting channel catfish, carp, and panfish usually come away happy as well.

This looker is representative of the much-anticipated shad run coming up the Delaware River each year.

Action usually begins in early springtime with the annual shad run. This has historically been a hugely popular attraction, bringing many anglers to the shores of the river, and even sparking a yearly shad festival. Both fly anglers and hardware tossers along the banks get their share, but the greatest success generally goes to those boaters who know the channel locations best, and use downrigging and trolling gear to keep their lures at the most likely depths. Although fish can often be found along the entire length of the river from Delaware Bay toward New York during the run, the greatest mass of fish tend be in one area at any given time as they gradually make their way north. A telephone hotline and one or two Internet sites have been set up to allow anglers to track the school's progress toward the targeted spawning grounds.

Striped bass action is generally associated with May, coinciding with their spawning activities, but in truth there can be great angling for this striped battler well into summer and autumn. It's prudent to start your search with some recommendations from local tackle stores; with these as your starting points, look for long, deep pools and their nearby flats, pinched riffles, and strong runs. Any eddies beside these are worth some casts as well. Although many of the specimens are on the small side, don't get caught with your pants down—the odd fish exceeds 3 feet in length and gets well into double-digit poundage.

As spring warms toward summer, smallmouth bass becomes quite popular, and for good reason. Numerous, vigorous, challenging yet catchable, and widespread, the bronzebacks of the Big D have accounted for more satisfying evenings for me and my fly rod than I can count. Look for almost any area with fast water and riffles, or even just a rocky bottom, and chances are excellent you'll have found good smallie water. A huge variety of baits will score on these muscular fighters; small baitfish, worms, hellgrammites, and crayfish top the list for natural baits. Lure wielders will do well with jigs, spoons, spinners, spinnerbaits, and crankbaits, and fly anglers see action with poppers, dry flies, nymphs, and streamers.

Another popular springtime target is the muskellunge. The Delaware River is the oldest location in the state for this beast of near-mythical proportions (all other lakes and reservoirs with this toothy monster have only been established within the past decade or so), and for many it remains the prime Garden State location to catch a muskie. The Delaware Water Gap and areas north see the most activity, and fish are hooked most often in places where you can find alternating deep and shallow sections, tributary intersections, and areas with current breaks: downstream of islands, large rocks, bridge pillars, wingdams, and the like. If you can find anything meeting this description with healthy weed beds, give it that much more attention.

Many warm-weather anglers spend low-light periods waiting for carp or channel catfish to take their bottom-placed natural baits. In the case of the former, success is maximized either by fishing areas with a known presence of the big-scaled hulks, or by chumming the area with dough baits or corn kernels (check for local regulations first) in advance of fishing there. Carp prefer slower- or still-water areas, whereas catfish may be found where there is some current as well. For both, look for spots with softer or even muddy bottoms.

Panfishing opportunities exist pretty much throughout the season, and a variety of sunfish, rock bass, and others will willingly smash an angler's worm. Some of the great advantages of this sort of angling are its simplicity, ease of success under most conditions, and the chance of something unexpected (read: bigger) coming along and grabbing the bait.

As the weather cools into midautumn and winter, walleye angling comes on strong. Although these goggle-eyed denizens can be caught year-round, it's during the colder months that most of the really impressive catches are made. High-water periods can be especially productive, particularly as the water level is increasing—but be sure to exercise due caution at these times, of course. After sudden increases in water levels, when current seems unusually violent, angling right along the banks can be highly productive.

There are numerous areas and access points along the Delaware River where you can fish from shore, wade into the water, or launch a boat. Some of the most popular include:

- Delaware Water Gap National Recreational Area, including Depew (Old Mine Road, 9.3 miles north of the gap), Poxono (about a mile south of Depew), and Kittatinny Beach (below the I-80 bridge).

- Worthington State Forest, Old Mine Road in Hardwick, a few miles north of the I-80 bridge.

- The Belvidere access in Warren County, downstream from the Belvidere Bridge.

- The Phillipsburg Boat Ramp, in Warren County on Riverside Way near the bridge.

Musconetcong River

Originating with Lake Hopatcong, the Musconetcong River system stretches across much of northwestern New Jersey, bordering Morris, Warren, and Hunterdon Counties, until it finally coalesces with the mighty Delaware River. Along this great length you can find a tremendous variety, and many styles, of fishing. It is best known, however, for its trout opportunities.

The program begins for most anglers in April with the annual trout stocking, which is very generous. During this period, going through May, these salmonids are the primary quarry. Fishermen seek them at this time with a wide range of offerings: live bait (mealworms, garden worms, salmon eggs, corn), lures (small spinners and spoons), and artificial flies (usually nymphs and streamers).

As the spring comes into fuller bloom and the water continues to warm, other fish begin to get more active. Smallmouth bass have a smaller but dedicated following, and productive offerings include medium-to-large worms, live baitfish, and crayfish. Small crankbaits (especially crayfish look-alikes), plastic worms, and spinnerbaits score with measurable frequency, and fly rodders can be successful with larger-sized nymphs, streamers, and surface popping bugs.

These bass are often hooked unexpectedly while anglers are targeting trout or panfish. Panfish are quite plentiful along the river's length, and as a rule they are not difficult to catch— simply dangle a mealworm or earthworm on a small hook in the water, and your efforts should bear fruit. Concentrate your efforts here in slower, calmer stretches of the river.

To round out the menu, there are any of a number of so-called rough fish that don't usually get much of the limelight. The "Musky" has plenty of these, too, and they have some charms in their own right. Chubs, eels, and suckers are representative of this group. The occasional pickerel, carp, and catfish are caught from the river as well, although probably not as frequently as the others described. All in all, however, the presence of over a dozen species of fish should be enough to provide angling pleasure for almost everybody.

The river flows through a variety of public and private areas, and much of your time will be spent within Morris County, although as the river flows along the southern border

of Warren County all the way to the Delaware, there are
plenty of productive areas. Of the many spots worth your
attention, a few are:

• The King's Highway Bridge (Beattystown) over the river,
near Route 57.

• The Seasonal Trout Conservation Area (see special regulations), from the Penwell Road Bridge (near Hackettstown)
down about a mile to the Point Mountain Road Bridge.

• Stephens State Park, near Mount Olive.

Passaic River

The Passaic River is kind of a funny place. It doesn't seem
like too long ago that it was listed as one of the 10 most pol-
luted rivers in the United States, but it has rebounded
admirably. It now hosts a fairly diversified and productive
fishery from its headwaters in Morris County to its endpoint
at Newark Bay.

Let's begin with the former. In Jockey Hollow (in
Morristown National Historical Park, near Mendham and
Harding), the quality and habitat are surprisingly good and
have earned a place in the state's Wild Trout program, promising conditions sufficient for resident trout to reproduce. As
such, artificial baits only are allowed, and the fly angler with
lightweight gear can have an outstanding session. The stretch
begins at the river's source and continues to Route 202.

As the water continues downstream, going through the
Great Swamp and then following the Morris County border
along Union and Essex Counties, it gathers some strength.
Along this stretch some leftover trout can be caught, along
with some smallmouth and largemouth bass, and this continues until the Dundee Lake section in Paterson (between I-
80 and the Garden State Parkway). By the time you've
reached this point, you will have already covered some prime

northern pike areas; popular spots for these toothy guys include the area where the Pompton River comes in (Two Bridges area near Fairfield), near the Willowbrook Mall, and behind Kennedy High School in Paterson. Another stretch attracting those in the know encompasses the waters just downstream of the Great Falls (look for the Great Falls Park on a Passaic County map) and the parkside stretches upstream from there, including spots along Westside Park and Pennington Park. In fact, anyplace you can gain access to the water along this beat, from the town of Little Falls well into Paterson, is likely to put you onto a worthwhile fishing hole.

Although some anglers do well with artificial lures for bass and pike, most of these fish are caught on live bait; herring and shiners are considered the best choices. From the heart of Passaic County until well into Essex, carp and catfish are also great favorites of local anglers, with some impressive specimens in the former family reported on a regular basis. Large worms are the favorite for catfishermen, while dough baits remain at the top of the heap for those big-scaled bottom dwellers. Another good area to try some of these is the river section paralleling Route 21 in Wallington, East Rutherford, and Rutherford; some parks along here make access that much simpler. Also check out West Essex Park, which follows much of the river as is flows along the Morris and Essex County borders.

From Dundee Lake down to Newark Bay, you're most likely to see carp, herring, and some striped bass. Stripers caught here are mostly on the diminutive side (compared with the species average, that is) but a few impressive specimens have been hooked each season in recent years. And if you let your bait trail along the bottom long enough, you could even pick up a stray crab or two.

Pequest River

In one respect, this river may the best known of the northern New Jersey trout waters, if only because it is home to the

Pequest Trout Hatchery. It has some great trout habitat and marvelous scenery to inhale between strikes, and don't be too surprised at the occasional smallmouth or largemouth bass, sunfish, creek chub, or sucker.

Access is very easy along much of its flow, from east of the hatchery all the way to its confluence with the Delaware River. And as far as baits go, if you like it, use it—they're all legal here. Natural offerings like fathead minnows, earthworms, and mealworms are best; salmon eggs produce as well. Small to midsized lures, especially spinners, are also effective, and favorite fly patterns include caddis- and mayfly-imitating dry flies, emergers and wet flies of almost any small and dark stripe, and standard nymphs, particularly those mimicking immature caddis forms.

Bring those chest waders to make the most of this river, although hip boots may suffice along some beats and in low-water conditions. Study the water before entering and map out an attack plan; it can make a real difference. Lots of different habitats, pockets, and configurations make this a different challenge from one spot to the next—which may be a mere 15 yards away.

Those fishing upstream from the hatchery should note that the 1-mile stretch from the Conrail railroad bridge to Route 625 (Pequest Hatchery Road) is a Seasonal Trout Conservation Area, where only artificial lures are allowed. Downstream from the hatchery, however, almost anything goes, and the fishing tends to be good, considering the excellent habitat and the presence of released or escaped hatchery fish. To try this productive spot, drive into the hatchery entrance off Route 46 in Oxford and immediately turn into the parking area on the right.

It's worth taking the time to explore the river's reaches as it courses westward; many anglers find that the best trout action occurs closer to the Delaware. One good area along these meanderings is right behind Hot Dog Johnny's in Buttzville, and the staff here have historically been generous in allowing anglers to park and get to the river. (It is wise practice, and agreeable to the palate, to patronize their establishment before or after your fishing.)

Ramapo River

It's hard to miss the Ramapo River in Bergen County. It enters from New York near Suffern, flows roughly parallel to and west of Route 202 through Mahwah and Oakland, and slows for a time as the Pompton Lake before it continues its journey southward. A surprising level of wildness characterizes this remaining bit of greenery in the most densely populated county of the state. Access is easy, it's well stocked by the Division of Fish and Wildlife, and when the fishing's done you can still hike, go bird-watching, and in general enjoy a day outdoors in a reasonably natural setting along a number of the flow's sections.

Trout are the primary target attracting anglers here. There isn't all that much in the way of a native population, but conditions are such that fish surviving the spring angling blitz can manage well into, and often right through, summer. As a bonus, other species that often cooperate include smallmouth bass, the occasional largemouth, and some pickerel, as well as panfish like sunfish and yellow perch.

As far as bait goes, you name it, people have tried it. Live-bait users score on the standard assortment of worms and salmon eggs; light-tackle artificial aficionados use spinners to good effect; and fly anglers produce with nymphs and streamers. Those who like to have some variety can tie on a small spinnerbait or crankbait to attract some of the smallmouth residents.

Access is easiest and most popular at the entrance to Ramapo Valley County Park along Ramapo Valley Road (Route 202) in Mahwah; simply park your car and follow the footpath in toward the river. It leads to a footbridge over the river, which is as good a starting point as any—if you want to get away from the crowds, some hoofing in one direction or the other (on either bank) will be in order, but there are numerous fish-holding spots in this region. Other popular access points include spots very close to the Route 17 over-pass, less than a mile north of the park; some people have reported success behind the athletic fields at Ramapo College just north of the park.

Rockaway River

The Rockaway is a surprisingly nice cool-water river on the border between eastern (or, if you prefer, crowded and urban) New Jersey and the less settled, more open western parts. It is accessible to a large population of anglers, yet retains many of its natural and relatively unspoiled qualities along much of its length. There is adequate opportunity to reach the water, and all manner of anglers—bait, metal, and fly—can gather here. Trout are the primary draw, and the Division of Fish and Wildlife stocks it generously with rainbow, brown, and brook varieties. River conditions are such that the trout population lingers through summer, and the occasional smallmouth bass comes to hand as well. (Although rare, some genuinely huge smallmouths have come from this river.) Sunfish round out the fare.

Most trout take real bait, especially garden and meal-worms. Those who mold PowerBait around small hooks catch some fish as well, and spinner-wielding anglers entice numerous specimens with Mepps and Blue Fox lures. As the season progresses, fly anglers find plenty to do also. Weekends are often better for parking, but weekdays have fewer anglers around; choose which evil is lesser. Although river access is good, conditions favor those who can get their feet wet, so bring along those hip boots or chest waders. Don't overlook small trouty-looking lies, like an isolated small boulder in midstream, because these often provide a haven that is overlooked by a large number of fishermen.

If you're approaching from Route 46 westbound, go through Parsippany and Troy Hills. Bear right onto Broadway

Avenue in Denville (there's a Japanese restaurant on the right side at that point), and you're on the river. Most street parking during the week is limited to an hour, so you may have to do some searching for a suitable place to put your vehicle. Another nearby location that attracts anglers is along Pocono Road, between St. Clare's Hospital and the intersection with Old Boonton Road.

Following the river farther downstream, past the Jersey City reservoir to its merging with the Passaic River, it loses its trout-friendly aspects but is no less fishable, now suitable for a mixture of smallmouth and largemouth bass, with a few stray pike and some carp thrown in for good measure. One easily accessed spot is right between Routes 46 and 80, on Old Bloomfield Avenue in Pine Brook. Of the numerous times I've fished this spot, I have never seen another angler but have invariably seen respectable (or better) numbers of bass—just be sure to bring some insect repellent, especially during late spring and summer. Good lure choices include crankbaits, spinners, and spinnerbaits; anything that moves or flashes is better due to the often stained nature of these beats.

Saddle River

Kind of the "poorer relation" of the Bergen County pair of rivers that locals like to fish, this river has nevertheless provided countless hours of satisfaction for numerous trout anglers. The quality of the water and environment are suitable for put-and-take trout fishing, and some occasional others like catfish, carp, or eels. Given the crowded conditions through which the river flows, you'll typically encounter plenty of trash—though it reflects the socioeconomic conditions of the area. It's simply a better class of trash. Look for empty Perrier water bottles and Java coffee pod packages.

The river will, however, yield up trout during the spring stocking period. Natural baits are always good, as are spinners and the usual complement of small hardware. Fly enthusiasts can also get in on the action; Glo Bugs, Hare's Ears, and other nonspecific patterns attract many of the hatchery offspring that swim within. In addition to probing the usual places—eddies, current seams and breaks, undercut banks—try using some of the floating junk as well; often fish will use it as cover. I've caught fish hanging out underneath some floating ply-wood planks in some of the slower sections.

Two primary areas to try are Saddle River Park in Ridgewood and Lake Street Park in Upper Saddle River; another is downstream from the bridge on East Allendale Road.

One final word: Would I recommend that you make a spe-cial extended trip here to sample the fishing? Perhaps not. On the other hand, there are undoubtedly plenty of spots for an aggressive explorer. There have been reports of fish found in pools well after the end of the stocking period, as well as some wild trout found in some of the small tributaries coming into the river. You can never be sure what you'll find if you seek thoroughly. That's one of the beauties of fishing.

Van Campens Brook

"To fish Van Campens Brook is to enter a time warp which can take you back a hundred years," wrote Al Peinecke in one of his contributions to the 1998 edition of *Discovering and Exploring New Jersey's Fishing Streams and the Delaware River*. As accurate a statement as you might find, but it is incorrect in one respect: There may well be more fish there now than there were a century ago.

Another one of the Garden State's Wild Trout Streams, the Van Campens originates in the southeastern part of Sussex County, in the Delaware Water Gap National Recreation Area; it flows southeasterly into the northeastern part of Warren County, and from there into the Delaware River. Swimming through most of this length are numerous small, beautiful jewels known commonly as trout. Fishing here can be extraordinarily relaxing, but with a due nod to Forrest Gump, relaxing is as relaxing does. Time spent here will recharge those psychic batteries while at the same time

The Van Campens Brook is just one of the streams in the state's Wild Trout Steam program, where an angler can find naturally reproducing—and unusually beautiful—trout.

ensuring a good muscular and agility workout, because much of the river makes its way through some heavily forested areas, making it a challenge to negotiate.

You're unlikely to find other anglers up to the effort, due to the lack of stocked fish and the prevalent size of those you're likely to encounter. Although some brown trout up to 16 or 18 inches have been reported from the lower stretches closer to the Delaware, you're far more likely to see much more diminutive tribe members. Think hand lengths; in some cases, finger lengths. But there are plenty of them here, and those you do bring to hand might make you squint from their bright colors.

There are two primary considerations to bear in mind while preparing for your trip here. One is size. Since your quarry has little in the way of excessive mass, and much of the stream is foliage-crowded, think light and short for your equipment selection. Spinning outfits can be ultralight and hypershort, with 2-pound-test line being more than enough.

Fly gear should be similarly short and light. The second consideration is stealth: The fish here tend to spook easily due to their small stature and relative isolation, so even the slightest disturbance can put them into an elevated DefCon mode.

Turn off Interstate 80 right before you get to the bridge over the Delaware; the turnoff brings you to a long-interval traffic light on Old Mine Road. Go right and follow the road for some miles to get to the Van Campens Brook area. The simplest access is a small park area on the right side, well marked, with the brook running right through it.

Wanaque River

This Passaic County drainage system may be better known for the impoundments it contains, most notably Greenwood Lake and the Monksville and Wanaque Reservoirs, but the two Wanaque River sections, upstream from Monksville and downstream from the Wanaque Reservoir, have fishing opportunities in their own right. The primary of these areas is the first, which flows through the Wanaque Wildlife Management Area in Hewitt and Awosting, ensuring good public access. (Discussion here will apply also to the lower part of the river south of the Wanaque Reservoir, but access is much more restricted. Like any other hurdle, however, this has the potential for providing premium action if you're willing to search beyond the obvious.) Trout tend to account for most visiting anglers during April and May, but those in the know are aware of the walleye, smallmouth, and even muskellunge opportunities that exist here, in large part due to population overflows from the waters north and south of this stretch.

Not unexpectedly, the majority of the trout caught come preferentially to natural baits, but a skillfully worked spinner can do a good amount of damage. Fly anglers have a tougher time due to the prevalence of nearby trees and foliage; some anglers get around these obstacles by attaching flies to the their spinning equipment and adding a small bobber or casting bubble.

The Wanaque has a reputation as a put-and-take stream, at least as far as trout angling goes, and therefore many anglers limit their quest for the salmonid residents to spring only. But the presence of the occasional lunker trout indicates likely holdover potential, so summer and autumn anglers have a good chance of seeing some of these persistent fish as well.

CENTRAL NEW JERSEY PONDS, LAKES, AND RESERVOIRS

Hunterdon County

Amwell Lake

This unassuming water is the primary offering of the Amwell Lake Wildlife Management Area east of Linvale. It has about 10 surface acres of water, with a maximum depth of 12 feet (in a small area near the outflow of Stony Brook, along the southern shore). Much of the bottom is muddy, with some underwater and emergent weedy areas along the banks and a few patchy areas otherwise.

Most anglers visit it occasionally in spring to get in on the stocked trout, using any of the standard menu of baits and lures. The majority of this enterprise is conducted on land, although a few enterprising anglers use small boats to further their reach. A word to the wise: Use extra caution in your perimeter explorations, as much of the surrounding land is marsh and could pose hazardous conditions.

It is in midspring, however, that the pond's primary attraction comes to a head—namely, the largemouth bass. Uniformly described as "excellent"—and justifiably so—the largemouth population here is well worth the visit. There are plenty of them here, and many grow to respectable proportions. A variety of techniques will serve: soft plastics worked with finesse, natural bait freelined, spinnerbaits in any of a variety of retrieve styles, medium to large bass fly patterns . . . Go with those that best suit your particular style and taste.

The pickerel and perch populations here are scanty to nonexistent, but ice anglers nevertheless should be able to keep themselves occupied with bass, sunfish, and crappie coming to their baits or jigs. The sunfish and crappie can, of course, be caught during the open-water times as well with small lures and jigs, worms, and other popular panfish baits.

There is hardly any launch facility here, and small car-top boats (with or without an electric motor) can be a big help in getting to those offshore fishy spots. For those who wish to probe really shallow spots, a canoe is a good idea.

From the south, take Route 31 to the Harbourton turnoff and take the access road about 0.25 mile farther on the right.

Round Valley Reservoir

The Valley of the Giants—as Round Valley Reservoir is often referred to—deserves its nickname, as this is undoubtedly the top destination in our fair state for trophy trout. It's one of only a couple of places in New Jersey where you can catch

From the "Valley of the Giants," more formally known as Round Valley Reservoir, brown trout record holder Len Saccente displays his mammoth catch. The Valley also produced state records for lake trout and smallmouth bass. Courtesy NJ Division of Fish and Wildlife.

lake trout, and the state's brown and lake trout records (a 21-plus-pounder for the former, and a tackle-busting, 32.5-pound leviathan for the latter) also hail from these deep waters. The state record smallmouth bass, at over 7 pounds, came from here as well.

Another variety of rainbow trout, known as Kamloops, has also been introduced to the reservoir in recent years by the Round Valley Trout Association to enhance the trout-angling opportunities. The subspecies is characterized by its stocky build and what many describe as superior strength and stamina.

Although there are times when shorebound anglers can make a respectable or better showing for themselves, for the bulk of the year boaters have a distinct edge. Most of the successful anglers troll downrigged offerings into the depths of these clean waters (anywhere from 25 to 80 down), using a variety of natural and artificial baits that mimic the water's forage species. Jigging is another popular tactic for deep-dwelling denizens.

All anglers should also note that the water is managed as a Trophy Trout Lake, meaning that there are additional restrictions on the numbers and sizes of fish you may keep; consult the current freshwater fishing issue of the *New Jersey Fish and Wildlife Digest* for current information.

Bass-angling opportunities, for both largemouth and smallmouth, can be nothing short of phenomenal here under the right conditions, but tend to favor those who are better prepared. The water's topography and depths can make it a challenge to find the primary holding areas; spend some time on the water, or seek advice from the local commercial establishments. Too, both species often show a marked preference for natural baits (live is better, very lively is best), so those keeping a healthy bait supply at hand will have the advantage.

The other predominant species here are channel catfish (including specimens over 10 pounds) and sunfish; however, it's a rare person who comes to target these—a number of the catfish are taken as incidental catches while seeking trout or largemouths. Those who do seek them generally find little competition, and plenty to keep themselves occupied.

Like most larger bodies of water, Round Valley can seem a mite daunting upon arriving for the first time. Many anglers begin their initial searches for the trophy trout along the campgrounds (along the southern shore, across from the main access area), near the launch area itself, and along the north shore near the tower and east of the launch. Those who are confined to the water's periphery can nevertheless get a solid crack at good trout fishing, especially during early to mid-spring and again in mid- to late autumn. One popular spot is the launch area and its immediate environs (just be careful not to stray onto restricted areas).

The facility can be reached by taking Interstate 78 to Route 22 in Clinton, and following signs to the park. Electric and gasoline (up to 9.9 hp) motors may be used here.

Spruce Run Reservoir

It's impossible to talk about freshwater fishing in the Garden State without mentioning Spruce Run Reservoir in Union Township. Its size (1,290 acres), ease of access, and incredible variety of fish make it a destination with something for everyone.

It's tough to know where to start, so let's begin with trout. The Division of Fish and Wildlife dumps over 5,000 hatchery graduates before and during the spring fishing period, making this one of the popular species sought by fish hunters old and young. Rainbow, brown, and brook trout all get some play here, and most are caught on small natural or artificial baits. In the former class, earthworms, nightcrawler pieces, mealworms, fathead minnows, and salmon eggs are in widespread use. Those who prefer plastic, metal, or wood score on spinners, small spoons, and crankbaits. The latter two are also popular among those who choose to troll for their springtime trout. The lake is not known as a holdover water, so trout angling tends to slow down as the water warms toward summer.

Another popular victim here is the largemouth bass, and anglers generally do well, especially in spring and autumn. Baits that have been shown to be effective are soft plastic jerkbaits, plastic worms, a variety of crankbaits, and dark jigs with crayfish-imitating trailers. It's worth noting that the water level—never to be assumed, as the reservoir is often under manipulation and subject to prevailing rain patterns— can have a significant effect on bass-holding areas. As a rule, go deeper and/or farther from shore when levels drop, but it's necessary to be flexible.

Many of the northern pike caught from Spruce Run are taken during the winter, through the ice.

Smallmouth bass are present, but in much lower numbers than their wider-mawed brethren. One angler has reported that he catches one smallmouth for every 19 largemouths he hooks in this reservoir.

Many people come here for the northern pike, and small wonder. Herb Hepler caught his famous state-record trophy here, a mammoth 30-pounder.

The drawback is that his famous fish was hooked back in 1977, and although pike are still caught here on a fairly regular basis, it's been rare to see one pass the 15-pound mark in recent years. Live herring is probably the most productive bait used, and some pike are taken in by oversized spoons, crankbaits, and spinnerbaits.

While we're talking about the genus *Esox*, one of the pike's relatives calls this place home as well. The tiger muskellunge, a cross between the pike and a true muskie, was placed here in the mid-1990s, and for number of few years there were fairly steady reports of specimens caught. Occasional reports persist, so don't count these guys out. They may be caught while targeting pike, as bait selection is very similar.

Are you a rocket scientist? By *rocket* I'm referring, of course, to the hybrid striped bass population. The Division of Fish and Wildlife started stocking these insane gamefish in the early 1990s and kept up a steady stream in the years that followed. The result is a chance for anglers to hook one of the craziest fish that swims in sweetwater. Live bait is the preferred choice of most successful anglers, especially herring and shiners (in that order). Livelined, slip bobbers, or suspended deep can work; some anglers use a combination of these. In spring, some anglers manage a few fish on surface lures, but for best reliability be prepared with a good supply of lively baitfish.

The other two primary attractions here are carp and channel cats, with excellent populations of each. Truth be told, these may the largest fish you hook into while you're here. Some people make it their specialty to go after these behemoths; popular bait choices for the whiskered guys include stinkbaits, herring, and nightcrawlers, while those after the big-scaled denizens often opt for corn kernels, homemade corn or dough baits, and various offerings with fruit or fruit extracts in them. Finally, panfishermen will never get bored here, with sunfish, perch, crappie, and bullheads just waiting to take your bait.

There are plenty of places to begin the search for great angling here. Popular among largemouth anglers are areas close to the boat ramp, northern shoreline stretches, and the northeasternmost cove, where Spruce Run Creek and Willoughby Brook flow in. Those with a preference for bronzebacks can start near any of the rock walls, throwing jigs near and along any rocky surfaces, or running spinnerbaits in these spots. If pike are your quarry, it's public record that Hepler caught his record fish from one of the northernmost reaches of the lake, a spot that locals now sometimes refer to as "Herb's Point" or "Hepler's Cove." It's the cove just east of that where Black Brook enters the reservoir, and both of these are good pike locations.

There are multiple boat ramps here, and motors are limited to 9.9 horsepower. Those who don't have their own can rent one from the on-site rental facility. There is a daily entrance fee between Memorial Day and Labor Day. The entrance can be found by following Route 31 north from Interstate 78, turning left onto Van Syckels Road, and proceeding 1.5 miles farther to the park entrance.

Mercer County

Carnegie Lake
To visit this place is to associate with education and erudition. Princeton University class of 1876 graduate Howard Russell Butler approached his deep-pocketed friend Andrew Carnegie and asked him to finance a lake so that Princetonians could practice their rowing for competitions. Carnegie agreed; the lake was created in 1906, and the Princeton team was back in business. Years later, after World War II, no less a figure than Albert Einstein could often be found boating on these waters.

Over the past couple of decades, the Division of Fish and Wildlife has given some attention to the lake, and it stands today as a worthwhile cool- and warm-water fishing spot. The primary species in the 237-acre lake are largemouth bass, cat-fish, carp, pickerel, and some panfish. Tiger muskellunge have been added to the mix as well by the state, but the fishing opportunities for them remain limited at best. Overall, the 3-mile-long waterway is flat, with depths generally hovering between 4 and 6 feet, though a few spots feature an extra foot or two. It's a popular destination for local bass anglers, and was even in use for a while for local bass tournaments, though strategic placement of some large boulders—reportedly by owner Princeton University—has made it impractical to park a vehicle with an attached trailer. But car-top users can still access the water easily enough (motor use is limited to electric only). Try soft plastics along the shoreline structure and submerged timber, or topwater patterns at low-light periods and around bridge pilings.

Strangely enough, the Division of Fish and Wildlife saw fit to toss some full-strain muskellunge in here a few years back, but I haven't heard of any subsequent catches. If you hook one, let me know.

Head toward Princeton University, and look for Route 27, which parallels the lake for part of its length; the boat launch area may be reached from Route 27.

Gropps Lake

A small pond near White Horse, this unassuming 26-acre water is a real Jekyll and Hyde, sometimes seeming pleasant and cooperative and other times downright ornery. Some anglers turn up their nose and give the place a wide berth, while others go out of their way to test their skills here. Many complain of the stained waters; some have even made comments about strange odors. But the fact of the matter is that there is a sizable population of largemouth bass here, and they have given up their secrets to anglers who are willing to cross their t's and dot their i's.

Start with the usual places for bucketmouths, including overhanging bushes, lily pads, and any other emergent growth you may find, and bottoms with appropriate structure like rocks and irregular surfaces. Patterns that have been shown to work include Carolina rigs, tube baits, spinnerbaits, and carefully worked rattling crankbaits. If you like subtle lures like soft plastics, consider staying with brightly colored shades to help the fish spot them. Don't be too surprised to catch the occasional chain pickerel; you could turn up a few crappie and channel catfish as well.

If you prefer the latter, and his poor-water-quality associate the carp, then this is an excellent place; both of these species have good populations here. Other panfish—sunfish, yellow perch—complete the roster.

Don't expect to have a banner day here every time, but some of the trips will definitely be memorable. Boating in small car-top craft (electric motors only) is allowed. The lake is located in the V between Routes 524 and Interstate 195, near White Horse.

Lake Mercer

Respectable in size, access, and fishing opportunities, this is one of the featured attractions of Mercer County Park, near Mercer County Community College in West Windsor. The 300-acre lake is perfect for the small-boat enthusiast, and shoreline anglers do well here as well. (If you neglect to bring your own, and change your mind after getting here, you can rent a rowboat at the marina.) Largemouth and pickerel draw most of the anglers, and the preponderance of weeds in a number of areas makes it an ideal habitat for both. Some bass anglers favor the outside bend along the northern shoreline, more or less across from the boathouse. And there's plenty of vegetation along most of the banks that holds gamefish willing to engulf your natural or artificial offering. There are plenty of other species to occupy interest as well, including sizable catfish and carp, crappie (which often surprise the bass/pickerel angler by whacking a jig or plastic worm), sunfish, perch, bullheads, and muskellunge.

Yes, muskies. The Division of Fish and Wildlife has been actively stocking this water with full-strain muskies in recent years, and the varied depths (going down to 20 feet in places) and habitat allow these elusive predators to reach some decent sizes. Best bets for these long heartbreakers are oversized shiners and the standard big muskie lures.

The park is open during posted hours, but you can fish outside those hours with a night fishing permit—contact the Mercer County Parks Commission for more details. The park entrance is located along Route 535, also known as Edinburg Road or Old Trenton Road.

Etra Lake

This smallish lake, really not much more than a pond at about 19 acres, is nevertheless a pleasant place to stop over and get a quick fishing fix. Part of East Windsor's Etra Lake Park, it appeals mostly to youngsters and those with families; the sunfish will always be willing to cooperate here.

Now that we've gotten that out of the way, those interested in a multispecies challenge may wish to test their mettle here. Those depths conceal a fair deal more than just some sunfish; some of the locals actually go out of their way to pursue the resident largemouth population, with reports of individual fish up to 4 and 5 pounds—although most of those you're likely to encounter will be a pound or less. Some even frequent the shallow areas during winter, due to the relatively low incidence of ice-over, and still manage to pull out the occasional largemouth. The normal assortment of natural and artificial baits will serve, and some have reported high levels of success with blade baits. Other species worth a try include pickerel, carp, and bullheads.

Etra Lake Park is on Disbrow Hill Road. There is a parking area next to the lake near the intersection of Disbrow Hill and Etra Roads. Car-top boats, but no motors (including electric), are allowed.

Grovers Mill Pond

The continued eutrophication of this nice suburban-style park pond, part of Van Nest Park, prevents the water—and fishing—from improving, but it's still worth spending a morning or afternoon here to get away from it all. The town of West Windsor even provides a small launch facility to the water, capable of accommodating a simple vessel like a canoe. It is part of a combination dock-boardwalk that can also serve the nonboating angler well. The 28-acre water body, near Princeton Junction, is part of Bear Brook, which then flows into the Millstone River.

Primary species are, again, largemouth bass and pickerel. Both will chase down topwater lures during spring and to a somewhat lesser degree in autumn, as well as during the late daylight hours of summertime. Panfish enthusiasts will find a cooperative population of sunfish and yellow perch to occupy their time, and bullheads will readily strike nightcrawlers and chicken livers. Sometimes the algal bloom from late spring and into summer can give the place an appearance of—as one observer has put it—a Martian invasion (reminiscent of Orson Welles's famous broadcast from 1938, which used this locale), but if you can use your bait to punch a hole in the mat of surface growth, the fish below will be able to find your offering more readily. The park and lake can be accessed via Clarksville–Grovers Mill Road and Cranbury Road.

Peddie Lake

No doubt about it: Peddie Lake is an interesting place. Located in Hightstown, it represents the primary public fishing opportunity within that community, and as such you might expect it to be heavily used by local anglers. But in fact, such usage is surprisingly limited. The small, 12-acre spot is equally well experienced from shore or by boat; the two boat launches are best suited for those with canoes or other small craft—and don't be shy about bringing along your electric motor and battery. In truth, though, oars or paddles may be the best approach, due to the water's small size and the local denizens' tendency to spook, in part because of the shallow waters through most of the lake.

Even a cursory glance at this water will confirm that your primary fishery will be for largemouth bass, and results here can be surprising. Four- and 5-pound individuals are hooked here with unusual regularity, especially on baits that are offered vertically and deliberately. Jig-and-pig combos in smaller sizes and muted colors are preferred, and alternating techniques of hop-and-stop and slowly swimming the lures can result in high hookup rates. Fortune also favors those who can find areas with deeper water and the transitional areas between.

The not-uncommon side catches of chain pickerel provide plenty of evidence that these long weed-area dwellers are present in ample numbers, as are some crappie and channel catfish. The catties, along with their diminutive brethren bullheads, will also gladly engulf a choice bait offering like live shiners or cut baitfish, as well as a worm or stinkbait impaled on your hook. Those looking for numbers, or a low-pressure way to spend time with the kids, can concentrate on sunfish, which will respond to the usual small baits used to entice these cooperative fighters. For some variety, small poppers or nymphs on lightweight fly gear can account for good catches also.

The lake is located along Route 33, near the intersections of Franklin and Mercer Streets.

Middlesex County

Farrington Lake
One of the major attractions of central Jersey's freshwater destinations, this lake comprises one of the slower sections of a tributary to the Raritan River system, and has a good amount of both shore and boat access (again, electric motors only) as well as a couple of nearby tackle shops. It has diverse habitats for a variety of fish species, and although well utilized it

never seems to suffer from some of the overuse that some other bodies suffer. This elongated water snaking through the landscape covers about 290 acres and has an average depth of only 6 feet, going as deep as about 20 feet near its easternmost section.

The majority of all freshwater species occurring in New Jersey can be found here, the notable exceptions being striped bass hybrids and smallmouth bass. The star attractions are largemouth bass, chain pickerel, northern pike, and channel catfish, with excellent panfish populations to appease anglers of all ages.

Live bait like shiners and herring will get you the fastest action on the largemouth residents, averaging somewhere in the 2- to 3-pound range, although there are plenty of bigger guys in there with reports of individuals getting as high as 9 pounds. Plastic worms are always good, and shallow- to midrunning crankbaits take their share as well. Bottom plumbers can try jigs, preferably in darker colors. After-hours adventurers have some success with surface baits including popping plugs. Incidentally, many anglers often visit a lake after dark partly to get away from the crowds, but often that's just when traffic on this lake gets going, so be prepared to wait at the boat launch if this is your plan.

One of the big draws in this lake is the northern pike population, and although the fishing for these water wolves here can sometimes seem hit or miss, when they're on, the action can be outstanding. Catches of fish in the 12- and 15-pound ranges are commonplace, and the primary baits to consider are large live baitfish—although a skillfully presented artificial (consider trolling with one) can pay substantial dividends. Pike are fairly widespread, but some areas that are named by local experts more than others include the area near Washington Avenue and the "Sir John's" ramp, as well as the weed beds in the upper, narrower end of the lake. Pickerel are abundant as well, and are often caught as by-catches while targeting either the bass or pike.

Another cooperative neighbor is the channel catfish, which often takes center stage when the bass and pike seem to be on holiday. Crappie are also popular gamefish here, succumbing to well-placed jigs near weed beds and emergent growth, or along any of the numerous laydowns and stony human-made structure.

Did I mention the trout? As though the existing fishing opportunities weren't enough, the Division of Fish and Wildlife stocks hundreds of hatchery trout in here before and during the first weeks of trout season each year. Most folks seek them from shore, and those targeting the other game species come up with some of these put-and-take fellows as well.

The lake is in North Brunswick. Start your access search by using one of the roads that goes over the water (Church Lane, Washington Place, and Davidson's Mill Road), all accessible from Georges Road.

Milltown Pond

Those who may want to avoid some of the traffic that can sometimes be associated with Farrington Lake can go to this diminutive, 10-acre spot a hop, skip, and jump downstream from Farrington. Shorebound and boat anglers (no motors allowed) can have a fine morning of fishing for the pond's more-than-adequate population of largemouths, pickerel, bullheads, panfish, and carp—although, if truth be told, you're most likely to see kids here dunking worms for the plentiful sunfish. Most of the youthful anglers station themselves at various places along the shore, as well as near the dam by Main Street. The pond is located in Milltown between South Main Street and Riva Avenue.

Plainsboro Pond

Described by at least one source as among the most popular places to fish in central Jersey, this place might not overwhelm you on your initial viewing. Yet fish in the 10-pound range have been caught here, including some very hefty largemouth bass, and the carp action can be very good.

Bass anglers have reported good luck with a variety of small soft plastics, and small, dark grubs are among the leaders in this tackle category. Some have additionally suggested that the evening bite is better than the morning, so time your visits accordingly. While you're casting, don't worry about missing out to the boaters—information from the Division of Fish and Wildlife indicates that boating is not an option here. Carp anglers have scored with worms, corn kernels, bread balls, and a variety of other dough-based baits. The menu is rounded out with a substantial sunfish and bullhead population.

Water's Edge Park borders the pond's north shores, allowing for simple accessibility. It's located in Plainsboro, on Edgemere Avenue and Pond View Drive, near Plainsboro Road.

Westons Mill Pond

At 92 acres, this is actually simply another section of Lawrence Brook that expands enough, and slows enough, to provide some good fishing opportunities. (The other primary waters along this length are Davidsons Mills Pond, Farrington Lake, and Milltown Pond before the brook joins with the Raritan River.)

Vegetation, including both submerged and emergent weeds, is an important characteristic of this water, and that should signal in your mind the following two words: *chain pickerel*. Indeed, the population of these popular and uniquely New Jersey esocids is extensive in this water. They'll go for almost any bait that's well presented (and often even if the presentation is something less than perfect as well): Natural, and especially live, offerings like shiners and worms are number one choices, while proven artificial lures include soft plastic (grubs and jerkbaits), topwater poppers and chuggers, and crankbaits. Largemouth bass will often show a fondness for some of these as well, but their numbers here aren't quite

Most anglers know the catfish as a spring and summer staple of fishing in New Jersey, but they can turn up practically anytime, like this fellow caught through the ice.

as plentiful—if bucketmouths are your primary target, then nearby Farrington may be a better place for you to spend some time. Don't overlook the carp angling here, either, as plenty of fishermen hook up with hefty specimens responing to their corn or dough baits. Bullheads, perch, and sunfish are the other varieties likely to grab an impaled garden worm.

One other species is worth mentioning here, and that's the tiger muskie. These big and exciting fish were stocked here in the early and mid-1990s. It's possible that you may hook into one, but reports of such catches in recent years have not been forthcoming, so this should be considered a low-probability enterprise at best.

Boats and motor are allowed, as long as the latter are limited to electric models. For years the boat ramp has been a source of some disgruntlement among those wishing to explore the waters; suffice it to say that your best approach is to stick with smaller vessels like johnboats and canoes. Head for Ryders Lane; if you approach along this road from Route 1 (you'll be going through Rutgers University at this point, as the water borders North Brunswick), look for Lakeside Drive and the dirt parking area and put-in point at the end of the road.

Monmouth County

Lunker Bass Lakes

Assunpink Lake is one of five lakes in New Jersey that, as of this writing, are designated as Lunker Bass Lakes. (The others are Parvin Lake, Delaware Lake, Splitrock Reservoir, and Boonton Reservoir.) This increases the minimum size of any fish that an angler is legally entitled to retain to 15 inches (instead of the minimum in non-LBL waters of 12 inches), and reduces the daily creel limit to two. The regulations are intended to enhance the population of trophy-sized bass in these waters, further increasing the recreational opportunities therein.

Assunpink Lake

This is a popular destination, and in some ways has an advantage over other waters in New Jersey, especially during the dog days of summer. A number of underground springs feed the water, in addition to the area's normal inlet system. This accomplishes two things. First, it makes the water significantly less subject to the ravages of the droughts that hit the area all too often. Second, the springs tend to keep the water a few degrees cooler than other spots, allowing the fish to better fight off those summer doldrums that can slow down angling.

If you like big bass, then a visit here is well worth your while. This lake has about 225 surface acres, with an average depth of about 5 feet (maximum 14 feet), and it will test your skill against big, heavy battlers. Largemouths in the 6-pound class are reported here regularly. Different presentations work for different people, but some baits that have proven track records are rattling crankbaits and live baitfish during the early season. Jigs, plastic worms, and buzzbaits come into play during summer. As the weather cools toward autumn, jigs, crankbaits, and Senkos will produce. Some areas that are popular during warmer months are the stretches across from the parking yard, the somewhat deeper channels, and shallower weedy spots. Assunpink Lake is managed as a Lunker Bass Lake, conferring additional restrictions on bass harvest; see the sidebar. Chain pickerel prowl these depths in great numbers, too, and are more than willing to compete with the bass for your bait.

Probably the number two quarry here is the channel catfish, and for sheer size they have the largemouths beat. Anglers often see specimens between 12 and 15 pounds; Magic Bait products like King Kat Chicken Blood are popular, and other natural and scented baits have produced many a bewhiskered victim as well. Although nighttime and low-light conditions are often preferred for the channel cats, many an unwary individual has been hooked when the sun is high. And boaters don't necessarily have the advantage; many of the catties caught here are taken by those fishing from the bank.

The other big story for Assunpink is the crappie fishing. Anglers regularly bring home *sac au lait* (a Louisiana nickname for crappie) that are over a foot long. To target these delectable and handsome fish, look for areas with a good amount of underwater structure, and use proven baits like crappie jigs or fathead minnows. Other panfish that will respond to a little coaxing include sunfish and perch.

Boaters need no longer complain about the primitive launch facilities here. Instead of the old dirt ramp leading to the water, a concrete ramp with dock has been installed recently, and the parking improved as well. Parking and launching facilities for both car-top and trailered boats are available at the access site off the Clarksburg–Robbinsville Road, in the Assunpink Wildlife Management Area in Upper Freehold, in the southwestern part of the county.

Manasquan Reservoir

The jewel of Monmouth County, this deservedly popular water, all 720 acres of it, is run by county authorities and is the major attraction of this park area. It has a productive and varied fishery, with a good variety of depths and habitats. But like any jewel of high value, it comes at a price—in this case the regulations surrounding the reservoir's use. The lake is electric-motor-only, and there have been lots of stories of park rangers who enforce this ordinance very passionately: asking people to remove the propellers from their gas-powered outboards, requiring people to have, and wear, personal flotation devices (under penalty of a monetary fine for noncompliance), showing boat registration papers at the launch site, paying a launch fee (available daily or as a season-long permit), chasing wading anglers from the water's edge, restricted entry hours . . . In short, it pays to contact the park in advance and get a complete list of the rules before going.

The other price to pay is the competition. This isn't exactly a secret honey hole, and during prime time in spring and summer there will be plenty of other anglers trying for a chance at one or more of the lunkers. But if you can be here during off-hours (like on a nonholiday weekday), and you've done all your regulatory homework, chances are good that you'll have a day to remember.

Let's start with the bass population. Most outdoor writers place this reservoir on their "Top Five" list of bass waters in New Jersey due to the near-astonishing regularity with which 4-, 5-, and 6-pound largemouths are caught here. The smallmouth fishery is probably the best one outside the northern reaches of the state. If you're used to fishing the run-of-the-mill bass pond, hammering the shallow water, using fast-moving lures, and the like, then chances are good that you'll get your share of bass—but not the lunkers. Many veteran anglers here agree that some of the real bragging-sized moss-backs suspend in the deeper waters, often in and near the submerged brush and timber, and to get to them you'll have to use some kind of vertical presentation. The "big 'uns" can be found in shallower spots at times, but if you're specifically targeting them, you'll have to adjust accordingly.

When you get tired of fighting big bass, there are lots of other species that call this place home, and one that gets the adrenaline going for more than one visitor is the hybrid striped bass. Recent electrofishing activity here, as well as anglers' reports, verify some good-sized members of this clan here. Live shiners and herring are always a good starting point; swimming and topwater plugs generally hook their fair share during spring and low-light times in summer.

Channel catfish grow to impressive proportions here, with reliable accounts of individual fish in excess of 20 pounds being caught; chicken livers are a favorite, and worms, cut baitfish, and doughballs have caught plenty of tribe members also. Some of the bigger specimens spend much of their time in deeper water, at depths hovering around 20 to 25 feet.

Other popular species include chain pickerel, crappie, perch, and trout (stocked before and during the spring trout season). From the Garden State Parkway, take Exit 98 to Interstate 195 west, and then take Route 9 north in Howell. From there, make a right onto Georgia Tavern Road, then another right onto Windeler Road; look for the boat launch on the left. Those without their own vessel can go to the visitor center to rent a rowboat (with or without electric motor) or kayak.

Spring Lake

Ask your average Garden State anglers what comes to mind when you say "Spring Lake" and there's a good chance they'll start discussing striped bass, bluefish, and other popular marine species—all widely sought from this pleasant shore town sharing the same name. And deservedly so. But the freshwater opportunities are worth the effort as well. The lake isn't huge, at about 16 acres; its average depth is a bit less than 5 feet, going as deep as about 8 feet. Its waters are fed in large part from underground springs—hence the name.

A good variety of fish are available, including stocked trout in spring, largemouth bass, chain pickerel, channel catfish, carp, crappie, and other panfish—not a bad menu for a predominantly saltwater-mentality locale. The lake is surrounded by parkland, ensuring good access, and those with sufficient upper-body strength and gumption can use a small vessel (no motor) to assist in their angling effort. Look for the lake a couple of blocks east of the Spring Lake Golf Club and one or two blocks west of the ocean.

Stone Tavern Lake

Back at the Assunpink Wildlife Management Area in Upper Freehold, the second largest water open to angling there is this 52-acre, amoeba-shaped lake. Largemouth bass are easily the most sought-after species here, and success rates vary considerably from angler to another, from one time to another, and from one report to another. Yet it is indisputable that there is a very good population here, and the lake has other advantages as well: Access is easy (once you can determine which of the unmarked dirt roads to follow) for both shore and boating anglers; the surrounding WMA provides a relatively untrammeled and natural vista, providing for a satisfying experience; and its close proximity to Assunpink Lake make it an excellent backup location should there be too much traffic at the latter destination.

Stone Tavern's undeveloped nature can be both a blessing and a curse, as many bass anglers are accustomed to fishing docks, stone walls, and other human-made structures in their quest for more and bigger bass, and virtually none of that is to be found here. But brush, weeds, points, and other natural bass magnets more than suffice in the absence of development by-products.

One of the more productive approaches here is the use of jigs, especially near any tree lines you may find. Other baits that are likely to connect with some of the local denizens are soft plastics and spinnerbaits. The ever-present chain pickerel is here as well and is just as likely to engulf your bait as the bass are, especially if you work the weedier areas. Those who wish to up their score on these elongated predators are well advised to try live shiners, either freelined or under a bobber.

One of the better, and less utilized, fisheries here is for channel catfish. The Division of Fish and Wildlife has been stocking them here every couple of years since the early 1990s, and anybody targeting these smooth battlers generally ends up with a story or two to take home. The panfish population, consisting mostly of bullheads, sunfish, perch, and crappie, is reasonably good and provides an excellent diversion from the larger species.

There are two primary access points, both located off Stagecoach Road (Route 524) near Roosevelt. One is Roosevelt Road, an unpaved byway; access to the lake will be on your left. The other is East Branch Road, from which lake access will be on the right. Once you find the water, each area has an adequate launch facility and parking spots. Again, boaters are advised that electric motors only are permitted.

Thompson Park Lake

A pleasant way to add fishing to a family outing, this park (actually a converted horse farm, with various parcels added to the mix over the years) in Lincroft has a stocked lake as but one of many attractions; it's simply fortunate happenstance that the lake's bass angling is unusually good.

The 22-acre water is at the end of the park entrance, and the parking and boat-launch area are open to the public. Though it's managed primarily for bass, other game species are sunfish, yellow perch, crappie, and bullheads. Think of it as an expanded bass-and-sunfish place, with the other panfish varieties put in for good measure.

From the Garden State Parkway (Exit 109), take Route 520 (Newman Springs Road) west for a couple of miles, and look for the park entrance on the left across from the Christian Brothers Academy. The lake has adequate parking nearby, as well as a working boat launch. Electric motors are permitted.

Somerset County

Best Pond

This is the sort of pond that's easy to bypass without a second thought. And frankly, that can serve you well, since you're more likely to have it to yourself. It's right next to bigger and somewhat better-known Watchung Lake, in the town of Watchung. Both are located right at the side of a local road, so they have no place to hide.

But there are two stories to tell at this diminutive water, scarcely coming in at 6 acres and located in an unassuming parklike setting, and the first is carp. This underdog of a fish, still with relatively few adherents in the United States, is so well represented here that some people make special trips to Best Pond for the opportunity to tangle with one of the burlier of these local denizens, with reported sizes of up to, and possibly exceeding, 25 pounds. Try to land something like that on your lightweight bass rig!

Most of the shoreline is available to on-foot anglers (boating is not an option here). One area worth a repeat try is the side of the pond aligned along the road, close to the willows. If you go during the late-April-to-May time period, there's a good chance you'll see some largemouth spawning activity, and this is Story Number Two: the water's largemouth bass. If you do happen to hook any of these specimens (and some go to about 5 pounds), be aware that both legal regulations and ethical angling practices dictate that any such bass caught must be immediately released during this spawn period.

There are plenty of largemouth bass, as well as a host of other varieties of fish, swimming in central New Jersey ponds.

And, to be sure, if the carp or bass decide to spurn your offerings for the day, there's always a respectable population of pickerel and panfish (sunfish and bullheads) that can provide entertaining diversion. Best Pond is located just east of Watchung Lake, past the Watchung Circle and along Route 527 (Valley Road). There is parking available just below the pond's dam.

Colonial Park Ponds

I've lumped three ponds together, since they're all located in the same place—Colonial Park in Franklin Township—and have similar fishing characteristics. The largest is Spooky Brook Pond, at 13 acres, and of the three this one also has the unique characteristic of being on the state's trout stocking schedule, receiving a few hundred hatchery trout prior to the April trout opener. (Actually, this is the only lentic water in the entire county that receives stocked trout.) The other two are 6-acre Powder Mill Pond and the smallest, Mettlers Pond, at a mere 3 acres.

All three have good shoreline access, and authorities have no problem with launching a small car-topper into Spooky

Brook or Powder Mill Pond. Anglers are, however, restricted to the bank at Mettlers. All of them have good fisheries in the largemouth bass and crappie departments, with respectable showings for chain pickerel. Best recommendations are to target these early in the morning, to take advantage of the low-light "magic hour" and also to give them as much as a rest as possible from the previous day's onslaught. Sunfish are also numerous here, and these feisty little fellows will cooperate pretty much throughout the day.

Spooky Brook and Powder Mill Ponds have the added attraction of channel catfish, and if you only have time for one of these two spots in your quest for Big Brown, try Spooky Brook Pond, which is stocked more frequently by the Division of Fish and Wildlife.

The entrance to Colonial Park is on Amwell Road; look for Mettlers Road and follow it into the park. Turn right onto Colonial Drive; Parking Area B will be on the right, providing access to Mettlers Pond. Farther along Colonial Drive are Parking Areas C and D; these are close to Spooky Brook Pond and Powder Mill Pond.

Watchung Lake

Located close to Best Pond, this larger water (at 15 acres the biggest in the county) started life as a swimming club and was purchased by the town of Watchung in the 1990s. The surrounding area converted to a park, very popular among the residents. Stocking programs have established nice fisheries, with the primary draws being largemouth bass and pickerel, and including good opportunities for carp, channel catfish, and panfish as well.

The entire periphery is open to shoreline angling only, and bass and pickerel will come to a variety of live and artificial baits, although in many cases they respond more readily to the plastic or metal versions than to the naturals. Spinnerbaits and soft plastics are good items with which to start, and anyplace where you can find some structure to which bass can relate—like any of the small points, and the wall—will generally yield more satisfactory results. Angling here is catch-and-release only, which provides even more reason to go with artificial baits where possible. (Although carp have on occasion been known to take a lure, the way to go for these big-scaled guys is corn, fruit, and dough baits.)

The park with attendant lake can be found off Mountain Boulevard (Route 527) at the center of town. Parking is available on Stirling Road, which runs more or less along the northern border of the park, near the dam.

Union County

Echo Lake

There are actually two of these, both located within Echo Lake Park in Mountainside. They are designated as Upper and Lower Echo Lakes, and comprise 10 and 6 acres, respectively. Although they are linked both by location and by membership in the Rahway River system, they are proof that size can in fact matter . . . but not the way you think. Almost across the board, the angling opportunities—for numbers and varieties of fish—are superior at Lower Echo Lake, the smaller of the two. It is stocked with trout before and during the spring trout season, and has no fewer than nine species of gamefish swimming in its depths. The most plentiful tend to be the sunfish and the carp, and the late-spring opportunities for the latter can be impressive indeed. Channel catfish, largemouth bass, and pickerel are available to both natural-bait users and those who prefer artificial baits. The panfish selection consists of sunfish, bluegills, yellow perch, crappie, and bullheads.

A word to the wise, however. The park is a popular destination for a multitude of recreationalists, and the vehicular traffic coming through can sometimes be a bit overwhelming—one observer has opined that he doesn't believe that drivers will stop for pedestrians in any of the crosswalks.

Boats are available from a livery on a rental basis, and there is access for wheelchair-bound sportsmen as well. Take Route 22 to Route 577 (Springfield Avenue) south and turn right onto Mill Lane; continue on Park Drive, and you'll see the water. Parking areas are available on both sides of the road.

Milton Lake

In many ways, this waterway is typical of the suburban New Jersey landscape. Located within an area that practically screams *development*, this 10-acre pond is found in a park area of Rahway that allows you to almost forget that you're smack in the heart of civilization. Just downstream of a dammed reservoir, Milton Lake is part of Robinson's Brook, a tributary to the Rahway River.

Much, if not all, of the periphery is open to shoreline angling, although parts of the terrain are less friendly than others; some places require some good balance and the willingness to engage in a bit of cardiovascular exercise. Once you're there, however, the variety of freshwater opportunities is rather extensive. The lake's inclusion in the annual trout-stocking schedule, including both pre- and in-season events, ensures a good supply of hatchery trout in April and May. As this fishery starts to get eclipsed by the warmer weather, largemouth bass and pickerel come into their own, and this gives way to the other species present: channel catfish (there are reports of some very large specimens caught here), carp, crappie, sunfish, and bullheads.

Located close to the border of Woodbridge, the lake lies between West Lake Avenue and Midwood Drive in Rahway. One access point is along West Lake Avenue; look for the edge of the wooded area just before the houses near Stalewicz Lane, where you'll find an unmarked path leading to the lake.

Surprise Lake

Another denizen of Union County's park system, this 25-acre destination is located within the popular Watchung

Reservation and may in fact be the premier fishing spot in the county. Kids aren't the only ones who try their luck at the surprisingly worthwhile angling opportunities here, including some of the best carp and crappie angling to be had in the region. (Note, however, that there have been some reports of a fish-kill around early 2005—the result of runoff from the reservation's nearby horse stables—which may have negatively impacted the carp here, and possibly some of the other species as well.)

Come and spend some time helping your worm coax some of the resident bass and pickerel, channel catfish and crappie, and sunnies and bullheads. Shoreline angling is most prevalent here, but those with small car-top vessels can use these as well, although you'll have to make do with paddles or oars. The lake is on the border between Mountainside and Summit, in the northeastern portion of the reservation near Park Drive and Tracy Drive, as well as Glenside Avenue.

Note that another public water, Seeley's Pond, is also located within the reservation, and has some worthwhile angling possibilities in its own right, with chances to catch most of the same species as Surprise—with the bonus of stocked trout in spring. Seek it at the southwestern border of the area between Scotch Plains and Berkeley Heights, near the intersection of Valley Road, Sky Top Drive, and Diamond Mill Road. Anglers should also keep in mind that county regulations do not allow for ice fishing on any of the waters within Union County.

CENTRAL NEW JERSEY RIVERS AND STREAMS

Delaware River (Central Sections)

Angling in the farthest-downstream freshwater stretches of the Big D concentrates, for most anglers, on striped bass. To be sure, striper fishing can be excellent from the Delaware Bay all the way up toward northern New Jersey, but from the river's freshwater/saltwater junction (at the Commodore Barry Bridge in Bridgeport, Gloucester County, as defined by the Division of Fish and Wildlife) up to the Philadelphia area, striped bass are pretty much king, even though the majority of these saxitili are less than the minimum taking size. Popular baits are bloodworms, soft baitfish-shaped plastics, with or without jigheads, surface plugs like hard stickbaits and popping lures, and noisemaking crankbaits with either a tight or a wide wobble. Some launch and access points include West Deptford Municipal Boat Ramp (Center Street), Pyne Point Marine Services (North 7th Street in Camden), and the Pennsauken Boat Ramp (Derousse Avenue in Delair).

Farther upstream, one of the other primary target fish comes into prominence: the largemouth bass. These fellows, although prevalent in many river systems, don't much like hanging out in current like smallmouths or trout do, so they're best sought along banks, in backwater areas, and anyplace where they don't have to work so hard fighting the moving water. Weedy areas are prime, and they will strike any of a number of natural and artificial baits. Smallmouths are present as well, as are channel catfish and white perch.

Proceeding upstream into the area between Frenchtown and the Rancocas Creek, the most popular species include largemouths, smallmouths, stripers, and muskellunge (including tiger muskies, which the Division of Fish and Wildlife includes in its ongoing stocking program).

Professional bass angler Mike Iaconelli (2003 Bassmaster Classic champion and 2006 BASS Angler of the Year) grew up fishing the Delaware River and nearby waters.

Those targeting largemouths during late spring and summer can seek them at high tide in newly flooded spots that can be typi-fied by vegetation: marshes, lily pads, and other brushy areas. If you have a choice be-tween spots that retain some water depth at high tide, and others that are left high and dry, concentrate on the former. Although good fish-holding areas are very widespread, a couple where you can start your search are the cove bulging into Pennsylvania territory, across from H. Kenneth Wilkie Memorial Park in Florence, and the areas near Newbold Island in the northern part of Burlington County.

Muskie anglers have plenty to keep themselves occupied as well, between the full-strains and the tigers. The state record tiger, a 29-pound bragger, was caught from the shore in the area of Washington Crossing State Park (Titusville). From Trenton to Philly, the water is characterized by a wide, slow, almost lazy feel, but if you find suitable areas in the channel, cover-containing flats, and some of the tributaries (including the Neshaminy Creek in Pennsylvania and Rancocas Creek), chances are good you'll find muskies. The waters right by the town of Frenchtown also hold respectable numbers of these impressive fish. During the colder months, it also pays to look for warm-water discharge areas, and one that fits the bill is the Mercer County Power Generation Station in Bordentown. Farther north, try places like Lambertville and Bull's Island (near Raven Rock), both in Hunterdon County.

Good access points along here include the following:

• D&R Canal State Park (Bridge Street behind Lambertville Station, in Lambertville).

• D&R Canal State Park (Firemen's Eddy Access, off Route 29).

• Trenton Waterfront Park (off Route 29 in Trenton).

• Bordentown Beach (Park Street in Bordentown).

• Burlington City Boat Ramp (Tathem Avenue and Pearl Street, near Assicunk Creek).

Delaware & Raritan Canal

This canal system is great fun to fish on two levels. It has some excellent fishing for some prime freshwater varieties in a relaxed and unhurried atmosphere, and the locales through which it passes recall some of the area's rich history. The primary purpose of the canal—to provide freight transportation between the Philadelphia and New York City regions via the Delaware and Raritan Rivers—was of course long ago made obsolete, but the angling and recreational opportunities linger.

It's convenient to think of the system in two sections: the Feeder Canal, which runs parallel to the Delaware River from Milford (Hunterdon County) to Trenton, and the Main Canal, which goes from Trenton to the New Brunswick area. It's possible to fish pretty much the entire length of both sections;

the primary species that anglers target are largemouth bass, pickerel, some panfish (mostly sunfish), and carp. The Division of Fish and Wildlife plants some trout here and there in spring, most notably in one of the D&R Canal State Park areas near Lambertville. The division has also reported an isolated catch of a flathead catfish here, a species not native to this region that could have the potential to be destructive to other species. Flatheads can be distinguished from channel catfish by noting the tail, which has a white upper lobe on the fin and is not forked like a channel's, and the head, in which the lower jaw juts forward beyond the upper. (Anybody who catches one is asked to not return it to the water, and to contact the division as soon as possible.)

The canal is significantly wide in a number of places, and not all fish-holding areas are easily reached by shoreline casting. Many explorers opt to use a boat, although there are few locations designed specifically for launching watercraft. Another factor to consider is that gasoline motors are not allowed, although electric units are. Small V-hulls, johnboats, and canoes (with or without a squared stern) are well suited to plying these quiet waters. Those without boats can rent from nearby concessions in Princeton and Glassboro. Some areas with simplest access include state park lands near the Mercer and Hunterdon County border, Washington Crossing State Park, Cadwalader Park in Trenton, and state park lands just north of the intersection of Routes 1, 95, and 295.

Lockatong Creek

Don't give up on trout angling, even if you're not in the northern part of the state. Lockatong Creek holds some very good opportunities for trout pretty much all year long. The water is stocked liberally by the Division of Fish and Wildlife each spring, and reports of trout catches persist into the summer, autumn, and winter thereafter. It originates in the town of Franklin and wends its way sort of south-southwesterly, absorbing Muddy Run in Kingwood and finally spilling into the Delaware River in Rosemont.

Trout are, as I indicated, the primary fare, and anglers of all stripes can have a go here. The relatively untrammeled nature of much of the creek's course allows for a rich variety of natural forage, including aquatic and terrestrial insect life, other invertebrates like worms and crayfish, and small baitfish varieties; these will be your guidelines when opting to use fly gear or heavier artificial lures. Unlike many of the other trout streams in New Jersey, the Lockatong is not managed for any unusual trout regulations, so pretty much anything goes within the trout-angling boundaries. In the areas closer to the confluence with the Delaware River, smallmouth bass opportunities are very good as well and can provide a welcome change from all those pretty salmonids once you get tired of them.

Some areas worth trying include the following:

- The creek's intersection with County Road (Kingwood Road) in Kingwood.

- Near the mill located on Strimples Mill Road, near the northern border of Rosemont.

- The Wescott Nature Preserve, located along Raven-Rock-Rosemont Road (this appears on some maps as the Lockatong Nature Preserve in Delaware); access to the creek is via the loop hiking trail.

Anglers should note that some sections of the stream have fast water, and some real waterfalls (up to 12 feet in height), especially after a good rain—in fact, white-water enthusiasts have listed this river as one worth attempting in order to experience some Class III and IV rapids. Waders especially should therefore exercise all due caution when exploring this waterway.

Manasquan River

Saltwater anglers will immediately think of the flounder and other salty angling opportunities to be had in this fertile waterway, but in addition this place has some of the most exciting trout angling to be found in the state, and the reason can be found in four words: *sea-run brown trout.* Since late 1997, the Division of Fish and Wildlife has stocked over a quarter million brown trout here. Many of them migrate out to the Manasquan estuary, where they spend a year or two eating and growing, and some of them follow their instincts to return to the freshwater regions. By then they can reach a good size—7 pounds and sometimes more.

This is not a fishery for the fainthearted. Many anglers have waxed poetic in their descriptions of the unusual elusiveness and outstanding fighting abilities of these mysterious fish. Although only 100 to 200 have been reported caught, smart money has it that plenty more have been hooked but not reported. The entire trout-angling stretch of the river, from the brackish waters near the Manasquan Wildlife Management Area upstream to near Route 9, has potential for these silvery and deep-bodied fish. And just in case this isn't enough to pique your interest, the division also stocks a liberal number of trout during the spring season as part of its regular trout program; many of these fish hold over well past the summer doldrums. Bottom line: This is a heck of a place for trout all year long.

To bump up your odds of success, it's important to understand some characteristics of a sea-run's behavior. They tend to dwell in the salty or brackish water of the river system, and when there's a spike in freshwater influx, that often triggers their movement upstream in a kind of abortive spawning move. Since the primary reason for such an influx is rainfall, the best time to try your luck is a day or so after the rain. This gives the fish time to move into one of the fishable areas, and also gives the water a chance to clear up somewhat, increasing the chances that the fish can see what you're offering. Most of the higher catch rates have been occurring when the mercury levels are depressed—November seems to be prime, with January, February, and March clustered around the number two spot.

A large variety of baits will work, but the most consistent action has been with natural baits, headed by the ever-popular nightcrawler. Eggs and spawn sacs are also good choices, as are mealworms and small baitfish. For artificials, you might try jigs with small trailers, spinners, or crankbaits; fly patterns like emergers and streamers have produced on occasion. There are plentiful access points; some of the most popular are:

- Lightning Jack's Marina, downstream of the Manasquan Wildlife Management Area at 505 Ridge Road in Brick.

- Manasquan River Wildlife Management Area off Ramshorn Drive in Allenwood. A paved road leads to a sand road directly to the river. This is a primitive launch suitable for small boat, canoe, or kayak.

- Allenwood: Lakewood Road Bridge and Brice Park. The latter, just upstream of the bridge, has parking and shore access; a canoe or kayak could be launched here.

- Parkway Bridge: Accessible via a shoreline path that begins at downstream Brice Park or upstream Hospital Road Bridge.

- Hospital Road Bridge in Wall. Parking is found just upstream of the bridge. Facing upstream at the bridge, the left shore trail leads to a pool opposite the intake screen for the Manasquan Reservoir.

- Allaire State Park, Wall.

- Squankum Dam, located at the I-195 and County Route 547 overpass.

- Angler Access (also known as the Austin Property), part of Allaire State Park located off of Squankum–Yellow Brook Road. A sand road leads to a parking area with paths to the river.

- Manasquan River Linear Park in Howell. River access is available at Southard Avenue, West Farms Road, Ketcham Road, and Haven Bridge Road.

These areas will also serve you well for springtime trout fishing. In spots, you might also hook into an occasional pickerel, catfish, or eel, especially in the WMA and in Allaire State Park.

Raritan River

This is a very productive river system that can be arbitrarily divided into three sections. One is the main stem, which empties into the Raritan Bay in Middlesex County; much of the fishing along here is for saltwater varieties. Farther upstream, in Somerset County and beyond the intersection with the Millstone River, the two main branches—North and South—meet at (where else?) Confluence Reservation in Hillsborough. The North Branch comes in from its headwaters in southern Morris County, and this branch is known for some trout fishing and surprisingly good smallmouth opportunities.

Let's begin with the South Branch, known primarily as a premier trout-angling resource. It originates as the effluent from Budd Lake up in Morris County, and snakes its way southerly, providing some good trout fishing as it goes through the county. Two areas to try here include the stretch along Bartley Road through Four Bridges and Naughright, and the well-known Claremont Stretch (managed as a Year-Round Trout Conservation Area, with additional restrictions on bait as well as creel numbers and size) in Long Valley, which is the mile-long area upstream from the junction with Electric Brook; some of it flows through Schooley's Mountain Park, just north of the intersection of Route 24 (Schooley's Mountain Road) and East Mill Road.

The river then flows into Hunterdon County, through Califon, and soon enters the Ken Lockwood Gorge. The gorge runs for about 2 miles, and is considered by many to be the most picturesque fishing spot in New Jersey. The fishing is pretty good, too, although it's restricted to artificials only; the vast majority of fisherfolk coming here are utilizing fly equipment. Use the big rocks and boulders to your advantage,

The Ken Lockwood Gorge of the Raritan River's South Branch is considered by many to be the most picturesque spot in the entire state.

working the areas both up- and downstream from these obstructions. Along the more northerly part of the gorge, you can find pockets of deeper and slower water. The gorge is also managed as a Trout Conservation Area (see above), although it isn't unusual to hook into the occasional smallmouth bass. The access road may be approached from either north or south. The northern approach will be from the city of Califon, along Raritan River Road. The bridge over the water at Hoffmans Crossing Road will show you that you're close to the northern part of the area; the road parallels nearby County Road 513 (High Bridge–Califon Road). Southerly access, from the High Bridge/Readingsburg/Cokesbury area, is easiest from Route 639 or 641, each in turn available from either Route 22 or Interstate 78. Follow either 639 or 641 to its intersection with the other, continue west on Cokesbury Road, and look for the unmarked WMA access road to your right, just before you cross over the river.

Once out of the gorge, the water quiets considerably, but there's still good trout angling available as the river continues its passage through Hunterdon County. There are a number of public access areas through here where trout anglers can try their hand; these include the eastern border of the Spruce Run Reservoir property, near Route 31 in Clinton, the South Branch Nature Preserve near Landsdown, and the South Branch Linear Park near Flemington. It's worth noting that the water, while maintaining its good and catchable trout population, becomes more and more favorable for smallmouth angling as it wends its way downstream. It finally makes its way into Somerset County, where it joins the main stem.

The North Branch of the river has its charms as well. It begins its life as headwaters in the southern part of Morris County, then courses its way through Somerset County, where it meets its brother the South Branch. In the northern parts of its flow in Somerset County, the trout angling remains good. It is stocked annually—and heavily—by the Division of Fish and Wildlife south of the intersection with Peapack Brook in Bedminster. Right in this area the trout fishing will do you well, with plenty of fish biting all year, including well into wintertime.

Farther downstream, another spot to visit is the Miller Lane Recreation Area; follow Route 202/206 south into

Bedminster, turn onto Miller Lane, and take that to the end. Moving a bit more south, where Route 202/206 intersects with Route 287, is another easy access spot; parking is available here on the road or in a lot across from the river. Leave 202/206 at this point, and find your way to Route 22 where it goes over the river. The fishing here has its rewards; if the water conditions are a bit high, you might try trekking upstream a bit to find the fish.

Close to the main stem are a couple of spots where the trout fishing lingers, but chances are good you'll hook into some good smallmouth action as well. These are the river's intersection with Route 22, and the nearby North Branch Park in Bridgewater. Both offer easy parking and access.

By the time you're on the main stem of the Raritan, you'll be targeting bronzebacks for the most part; 3- and 4-pound specimens are caught from this region with fair regularity. Near the confluence is Duke Island Park, sandwiched between Routes 624 and 567 in Bridgewater; another good stretch is that which parallels Weston Canal Road in and near South Bound Brook. Farther downstream, the river becomes saltier as it gets closer to its terminus into the Raritan Bay. The border between fresh and salt water, at least as defined by the Division of Fish and Wildlife for the purposes of a freshwater license, is the Landing Lane Bridge in New Brunswick.

10

SOUTHERN NEW JERSEY PONDS, LAKES, AND RESERVOIRS

Atlantic County

Bargaintown Pond

Located predictably enough in Bargaintown, this 18-acre pond is part of the Patcong Creek and Maple Run waterway. Unassuming in its appearance and facilities, the pond nevertheless has a healthy freshwater complement dominated by chain pickerel and largemouth bass. The latter is a popular target of some of the local bass-angling clubs, which hold tournaments here on an occasional basis. Average size for this bassery is about 2 pounds; typical specimens come in at 13 to 16 inches. In addition, the casual angler will also find an unusually good panfish population, with plenty of crappie, sunfish, and perch.

There are few constructions here to help the angler, and boaters who wish to launch here will have to make do with somewhat primitive launch facilities, as well as restricting themselves to electric motors only. There is good shoreline access for the footbound outdoorsman. The pond is located near Linwood and Northfield, bordered by Central Avenue, Bargaintown Road, Lake Drive, and Zion Road.

Birch Grove Park Ponds

Smorgasbord time. The town of Northfield hosts this marvelous park that contains, among other offerings, a network of connected lakes—21 in total. None of them is huge—the total acreage among all waters barely reaches 30—but the layout makes for a good variety of access and structure availability. They contain a nice variety of fish, the two most popular of which are trout (stocked in spring and winter) and largemouth bass. (Note that Atlantic County residents have only this venue and Hammonton Lake available to them for trout, if they wish to stay local.) The latter are available in most of the waters. The lakes can be arbitrarily divided into three groups: the front lakes, the back lakes, and the others. The front lakes are characterized by simple access, with boardwalks and ramps for wheelchair access, and the back lakes are open to those willing to trek along the trails and over the small bridges to reach them.

Most of the waters are stained and have poor visibility, suggesting that those targeting largemouths stay with baits that have some color or flash. Slow baits seem to outperform the faster ones here, so stick with jigs, soft plastics, and the like over spinnerbaits and crankbaits. If you're up to the hike to the back ponds, they hold excellent populations of bass—some up to 5 pounds or so, although you're more likely to see most in the 1- to 2-pound range—as well as good pickerel numbers.

Sunfish and crappie are also present in good numbers, as are yellow perch, and channel catfish are stocked regularly by the division. The park hosts a number of local tournaments here. Boaters might seem stymied at first by the lack of obvious launch facilities, but anybody who can transport a small vessel in can use it with an electric motor. Fishing is also encouraged by the availability of live bait and some fishing tackle supplies for sale at the on-site refreshment concession.

From the Garden State Parkway, Exit 36, take Route 651, also known as Fire Road, south (via Tilton Road if coming from the north). Turn left onto Mill Road, Route 622. Make another left onto Burton Avenue and look for the park on the left.

Hammonton Lake

Eutrophication (an influx of excess organic materials, causing the water to become too fertile) has been an ongoing issue with this lake in Hammonton, and local authorities have been investigating methods to slow, halt, reverse, or mediate this condition. But the fishing continues to be very good here, as evidenced by the continued selection of the site by local bass-angling clubs for tournaments and the unabated interest in the notable pickerel population.

Trout fishing in this 75-acre water is a critical ingredient in the angling picture as well. This is the other of only two sites in Atlantic County for trout angling (see Birch Grove Park Ponds, above), which draws a good number of fisherfolk in springtime. Another important implication of this is that the trout apparently add to the lake's forage base, and local wisdom has it that they help the resident bass and pickerel reach larger sizes than they might otherwise. Taking this concept a step farther, more than one angler has reported success fishing for these species with trout-colored artificial lures.

Weedy shorelines provide good locations to try spinnerbaits and small crankbaits. Those with bass on the brain can also try the submerged timber closer to the eastern part of the lake; vertical presentations with jigs and weighted worms are the ticket. Crappie, sunfish, and perch are available, for sure, but don't overlook the catfish. Bullheads will come readily enough to your worm, and channel catfish are placed here regularly by the division and can grow to impressive proportions. Those who wish to keep any pickerel must keep in mind that the lake is subject to special regulations: All pickerel creeled from this water must be at least 15 inches in length.

The lake favors boaters, although there are some places where shoreline anglers can have a go at it as well. To reach the boat ramp, enter the Hammonton Lake Natural Area from Egg Harbor Road, and follow the entryway in to the ramp area behind the ball fields.

Hammonton's Unique Stocking Program

The rumor behind Hammonton Lake's inclusion in New Jersey's trout-stocking program is an amusing one. As the story goes, one of the Division of Fish and Wildlife's trout delivery trucks was en route to another location when engine failure forced it to a halt. As fate would have it, the driver found himself right next to Hammonton Lake, and—faced with the prospect of his cargo of trout dying—decided instead to dump them into Hammonton to at least give them a fighting chance at life. The addition did surprisingly well, and a new stop was added to the trout-stocking program for future years.

Lenape Lake

At 350 acres, Lenape is the big lake of the county, and it has plenty of excellent angling opportunities for the freshwater enthusiast. Rated as excellent for largemouths, pickerel, crappie, and yellow perch, it attracts anglers all year long. Individuals in the first two categories can be hefty, as local bass anglers have weighed in fish exceeding 5 pounds. The water is infamous for its stained reddish color from the resident cedar trees, and there is a good complement of woody cover as well as gravelly bottoms.

Wintertime anglers are particularly fond of this place due to the great perch, pickerel, and crappie (all good cold-weather species) opportunities; it's not unusual for a pair of January fishermen to hook 100 or more perch in a day. The lake's popularity for boating events also tends to hamper excessive angling traffic during the warmer months, and this situation simply doesn't exist in winter. Boaters can launch almost anything they have, although it's important to keep the

motor requirements in mind. All outboards must be pre-regis-
tered with the park; those in excess of 9.9 horsepower are subject to additional requirements. To avoid problems on-site, it's
best to contact the park authorities in advance of your visit.
Boating is also restricted to between 7:30 AM and half an hour
after sunset. Those without vessels can rent canoes from
nearby businesses in Mays Landing.

Some boaters unfamiliar with the lake have gotten turned
around, especially in the northern half, where there are
number of twists and turns and irregularly shaped branches
and coves. If you've been considering getting a GPS unit, this
would be a good place to use it.

The facilities are very friendly, and numerous visitors
have been generous in their praise of the well-kept comfort
facilities, park office, fishing dock, and boat ramp. The park
office and launch area are accessed off Route 559 north of
Mays Landing.

Maple Lake

This 35-acre destination is one of the two major features along
Stephen Creek (the other is Stephen Lake) before the latter
empties into the Great Egg Harbor River, and it's one of the
primary features of the Maple Lake Wildlife Management
Area, located in northern Estell Manor. Like most other
sweetwaters in southern New Jersey, it has a plentiful—outstanding, actually—pickerel population, and was stocked with
largemouth bass in the early 1990s; that fishery continues
strong today. Access is a fairly simple matter; bank fishers can
try their luck along Maple Avenue, along Burnett Avenue
(which follows the lake's northeastern boundary), or from any
of the areas into which they care to hike. (Keep in mind that
this WMA also has hunting opportunities; exercise due caution during hunting seasons.)

As in other South Jersey lakes, the pickerel and panfish
opportunities are excellent here, with very good bass fishing
as well. Typical sizes for the latter range in the 1- to 2-pound

area, but there is always potential for something significantly heftier. Small to medium-sized baits work here, with preference often shown for soft plastics and other slowly worked lures.

Boaters can use the launch ramp to put in their vessel; electric motors are allowed, but gasoline outboards are not. The launch area is on Maple Avenue, along the lake's southern edge.

Makepeace Lake

Big and wide, and studded with emergent foliage, sometimes it seems that Makepeace is just a swamp waiting to happen. Heck, you'll be hard pressed to find a spot that's more than a yard deep. But bring your canoe or johnboat and you'll find that it can make for a surprisingly pleasant day of fishing. (Electric motors are okay, but be sure to use a short shaft.) Pickerel are king here, and long casts are the way to go—it's too easy to scare the fish with your boat's motion. There's also a fair population of panfish, and the occasional largemouth bass. Most of the latter are, however, on the diminutive side and are not as a rule caught with any regularity. There are some bullheads here as well.

Look for Makepeace Lake near Hammonton and Mays Landing. Parking and launching are available on Elwood–Weymouth Road (Route 623), just south of its intersection with the Atlantic City Expressway. The lake is popular with some waterfowlers, who like to take advantage of the water's attraction for black ducks and wood ducks, as well as Canada geese; autumn and winter pickerel seekers are advised to keep that in mind as they paddle or motor about.

Burlington County

Laurel Acres Park Pond

Wilderness angling? Hardly. Almost the exact opposite, in fact. But this award-winning park in Mount Laurel offers a huge amount to do and is extremely popular among local residents. Playgrounds, baseball, soccer, stage presentations, volleyball, nature trails, and more await the visitor who needs some fresh air.

Not to mention fishing. The park set aside a few acres for a fishing pond, and stocks it regularly with trout. Largemouth bass, channel catfish, plentiful panfish, and more are also present in good numbers. Virtually the entire periphery is accessible to kids both young and old, and the fishing can be astonishingly good. Garden worms are the preferred bait here, with other natural baits like mealies, corn, and doughballs accounting for their fair share. Early-morning adventurers seeking to up their score on the largemouth clan often find themselves fighting unwilling adversaries who have engulfed their spinnerbait or plastic worm.

Access is close from South Church Street in Mount Laurel, a short distance south of the New Jersey Turnpike overpass.

Mirror Lake

In many ways the central fishing spot for Burlington County freshwater enthusiasts, this long and thin destination is part of the spiderlike Rancocas drainage system, situated near Browns Mills and northwest of Lebanon State Forest. Its 250 acres are predominantly east–west oriented, and appeal equally to those seeking largemouth bass, chain pickerel, and carp.

One of the favorites of area bassers, Mirror Lake is often the site of bass club tournaments, and for good reason. Many a five-fish limit is brought to the scales by tourney's end, and lunkers are often in the 5- and 6-pound weight class. Years ago the lake was known to only a handful of tight-lipped visitors, but word of good bass catches couldn't be contained; the lake sees more use nowadays. There's a good assortment of structure to probe, and largemouths may be found near the docks, in weeded areas, and where structural contours occur. (Those fishing near the docks are advised that there have been conflicts in the past between anglers and others using the dock areas; be scrupulous in observing the courtesies governing

Crappie are well distributed throughout the state, and the southern region holds some of the best opportunities for this tasty fighter.

multiuse areas.) Summer and autumn seem to have the most frequent occurrences of better bass-fishing days than does springtime. Jigs with trailers are among the more popular baits.

Carp, as mentioned, are worthy adversaries here, and the channel catfish population also merits some attention. Panfish will almost always provide either primary or fallback action, with generous numbers of bluegills, crappie, and perch present. Boaters can use the launch facility but are advised to exercise caution due to reports of a sharp drop-off at the ramp's end (contingent on prevailing water levels, naturally). Electric motors, but not gasoline, are allowed. Mirror Lake is located south of Fort Dix Military Reservation. Look for Route 676 circumscribing the lake; it is also called Lakeside Drive (with North and South branches).

Pemberton Lake

This 20-acre water will appeal equally to the boater or non-boater, in part because there are few areas with any kind of meaningful depth—in fact, you'll be hard pressed to find any spot that's more than a couple of yards to the bottom.

Largemouth bass are probably the most popular target fish here, with chain pickerel a close second and followed by the crappie and channel catfish possibilities. The areas with easiest access (along the roads) will provide action for both natural and artificial bait wielders. If you've brought your boat, the side of the island closest to the Colemans Bridge Road launch areas is worth some time investment, as the depth drops off somewhat steeply from that side of the island.

Boat launching is possible from either the old beach area (to your left after entering the area from Colemans Bridge Road), or farther along that entryway at the shallow cove. Either way it's necessary to use caution, and caution dictates use of smaller boats—besides, according the Division of Fish and Wildlife, no motors of any kind are allowed here anyway. There's also a parking area and dock at the northwest corner of the lake.

Look for Pemberton Lake at the intersection of Magnolia Road (Route 644) and Colemans Bridge Road, in the southeast part of the town of Pemberton.

Strawbridge Lake

The central feature of one of Moorestown's favorite public areas (Strawbridge Lake Park, of course), this 14-acre spot was actually known as Hooten's Creek until World War II, after one of the area's most influential families from colonial times. It was a popular fishing spot until the 1990s, when ongoing problems of shoreline erosion, sedimentation, and pollution finally took their toll. The New Jersey Department of Environmental Protection stepped in with a number of techniques to improve the quality of the water and its surrounding areas; these efforts have been highly successful.

A number of people remember those poor-quality days ("Strawbridge is long dead" is a comment typical of that thinking), but in fact the angling possibilities are definitely worth a try these days. Pickerel and bass (specimens up to 3 and 4 pounds are reported with regularity) are the top choice for those in the cool- and warm-water camp, while carp hunters do well here also, and panfish populations (sunnies, perch, bullheads, and crappie) provide plenty of backup action. Boating is open to those with small electric- or biological-powered craft.

The park is nearly adjacent to Route 38 (off Exit 40 from Interstate 295), and accessible via Haines Drive.

Sylvan Lakes

Upper and Lower Sylvan Lakes are found in the outlying parts of the town of Burlington. The former, really not much more than a pond at about 4 acres, has an average depth of about 7 feet and goes down to a maximum of about 15 feet. Lower Sylvan is comparable, with the most profound bottom at around 14 feet and with more places to probe, at about 14 acres. The two are connected by a ditch, used by local water authorities to drain Upper into Lower during high flow conditions.

One of the few places in the county where anglers can get their springtime trout fix, these waters are stocked both before and during the trout season. Of special interest here is the Division of Fish and Wildlife's "bonus broodstock" program, in which the water gets stocked with a bunch (usually a few dozen) of larger brooder trout individuals, allowing for a chance at some memorable stockies. Once the spring trout flurry passes, there are plenty of other species to catch: largemouth bass, chain pickerel, carp, crappie, yellow perch, sunfish, and bullheads.

Small watercraft are fine here, but leave all motors at home—although oars and paddles should be more than enough to let you explore thoroughly. Float tubes are a viable option as well. Close to the intersection of Sunset Road (Route 634) and Rancocas Road (Route 635), look for Sylvan Park Road, which will bring you to this destination.

Camden County

Blackwood Lake

One of the stops along the Big Timber Creek before it empties into the Delaware River, 25-acre Blackwood Lake is predominantly a shallow and weedy expanse best known for its historic carp and bullhead fishing. But don't overlook the largemouth bass here. Although many anglers describe the bucketmouth opportunities as limited at best, there are certain times when the action on these surly guys can be very satisfying. Two approaches in the artificial-baits category are topwaters and brightly colored or water-displacing lures. Both are preferred because of the usually discolored and often muddy condition of the water, allowing the sight-oriented bass a chance to zero in.

Some have reported better-than-average action near the dam at the northern end of the lake, with rumors of individual fish exceeding the 6-pound mark. To target any of these oversized leviathans, natural bait is an excellent choice (a good, lively shiner can't be beat). When you get tired of the bass action, or want to bypass the carp/bullhead bite, there are plenty of sunnies, crappie, and perch willing to steal a worm or two from you.

Car-top boats, powered manually only, will serve well here. The lake abuts the northern edge of the Camden County Hospital property, and can be accessed via Church Street in Blackwood, not far from the Black Horse Pike (Route 168).

Cooper River Waters

The Cooper River originates in the southeastern part of the county, and makes its way in a northwesterly direction until it meets with the Delaware River. Although it was described in 1990 by one government agency as "highly degraded," some cleanup efforts in the intervening years have helped significantly. Still, occasional advisories against consuming any fish caught from various stretches suggest that, at least for the immediate future, it might be best to treat all angling along this waterway as catch-and-release.

It is nevertheless fishable along much of this length, with recreational opportunities dominated by largemouth bass, pickerel, carp, and sunfish. Other species that have been reported include crappie, channel catfish, bullheads, and eels. There are a few places along its flow where it's been stopped up to provide some lake-angling opportunities. Traveling upstream from its Delaware confluence, the first such stop is the Cooper River Lake, located within Cooper River Park. The lake within is about 150 acres, and there's a launch facility to put in your boat (electric motors are permitted). It's located in parts of Cherry Hill, Collingswood, and Haddon, and is accessible via North Park Drive, South Park Drive, Route 130, and Grove Street.

Farther upstream you'll encounter Hopkins Park, whose 5-acre Hopkins Pond has a good variety of gamefish available, and is the only stop along the Cooper where you'll find put-and-take trout during the spring stocking season—in fact, one lucky angler won a New Jersey Skillful Angler Award during the 1990s with a nice specimen in excess of 4 pounds from this diminutive pond. Hopkins isn't stocked with trout every year, so be sure to check with the Division of Fish and Wildlife for the current schedule.

Those who like crappie action should consider this spot worth a special trip; bottom action for carp and catfish varieties can be unusually good here as well. This one is in Haddonfield, off Grove Street and on both sides of Hopkins Lane.

Wallworth Lake and Evans Pond are the next stop; these two are practically contiguous. The former is a mere 4 acres in area and allows only shore angling, although those who try it are generally rewarded with worthwhile catches of panfish and some modest bass. Evans, a bit bigger at 12 acres, allows small car-top vessels (no motors permitted), and some decent bass have been hauled from these depths, in the 3-

and 4-pound range; spinnerbaits tend to be favored here, especially early in the season. Wallworth Park is in Cherry Hill and Haddonfield, and is bordered by Kings Highway and Brace Road.

A few miles farther from the Delaware lies 26-acre Kirkwood Lake in Lindenwold. The often dirty and sometimes greasy water here can yield action ranging anywhere from ho-hum up to fairly good, dominated by bass and sunfish. Some carp, bullheads, and eel are caught as well, and smart money is on natural bait; nightcrawlers are always a good start. Look for Glendale Road, Washington Avenue, and Lakeview Avenue.

The last stop on our Cooper tour is diminutive Linden Lake, whose 3 surface acres may be attempted from the banks only. Panfishing is quite good here, and the pickerel and bass populations are worth some casts in their own right. The pond's small size means there are fewer places where they can stay out of casting reach. It's also located in Lindenwold, between Norcross Road and Jackson Avenue.

New Brooklyn Lake

In a few respects reminiscent of Lake Musconetcong in the north, this wide and weedy expanse harbors plenty of those long fish that love thick underwater foliage—namely, chain pickerel. Depth considerations are also similar: New Brooklyn never gets much deeper than 6 feet, and even that is a stretch in most places.

Live bait is probably the easiest and most productive—and certainly helps with the lake's bullhead population—but artificials can provide hours of satisfaction as well. Springtime anglers catch their share with topwater plugs, crankbaits, spinnerbaits, and buzzbaits; as the weather warms, slower finesse baits (soft plastics—worms, jerkbaits, and the like) can prove their mettle.

Shoreline access is good, but you'll be ahead of the game if you throw a canoe on top of your automobile before you travel here (no motors, please). There are a number of grassy islands scattered through the lake, and often good catches can be had in their vicinity; also try the deeper spot closer to where the Great Egg Harbor River enters. Fly anglers will find plenty of space in which to make unencumbered back-casts as they tempt any of the bass or pickerel to their streamer offering.

The lake is located in the southern section of New Brooklyn Park in Sicklerville, close to New Brooklyn–Cedarbrook Road.

Cape May County

Cape May County Park

This 200-acre public facility is best known for its well-maintained zoo (which—at least as of this writing—is free). But another good reason to come is the no-frills angling to be had at the surprisingly large pond on the property. Don't bother with any boats or anything else remotely fancy, but do bring that spinning gear and try your luck for any of the bass, pickerel, sunfish, or perch here. Garden worms are the easiest place to start; try small (4-inch) plastic worms if you prefer to concentrate on the largemouths or chainsides within. Bump up the amount of bait on the hook if any of the resident bullheads are more to your liking. The facility can be found at Route 9 and Crest Haven Road in Cape May Court House, close to Exit 11 off the Garden State Parkway.

Dennisville Lake

This is yet another perfect example of very fine sweetwater opportunities smack in the middle of saltwater territory. Located along Route 47 near, yes, Dennisville, many local anglers—as well as a bunch from outside the immediate vicinity—make a point of visiting a few times each season. The bucketmouths and chainsides here are both numerous and sizable, accounting for much of the attention. Spinnerbaits and other water-covering baits are popular during the spring months, and slower baits come into greater prominence starting in June. Natural baits—and don't forget those baitfish—are also well utilized here.

The Division of Fish and Wildlife has been stocking Dennisville with a significant number of channel catfish, and these skulking fighters have garnered more attention as a result. Commercial catfish baits are especially popular here. Don't forget the ample populations of sunfish and yellow perch, always ready to destroy a piece of worm dangled from a small hook. Electric motors on small boats are allowed; caution is advised, as the access point is very close to the main road (Route 47), which can be heavily trafficked.

This typical hatchery-bred rainbow trout is the quarry of untold thousands of New Jersey anglers at the beginning of April.

East Creek Pond

This is one of the two primary angling spots in the very picturesque area known as Belleplain State Forest—the name says it all. East Creek, all 62 acres of it, is no secret to the region's bass anglers, who come here for tournaments and just plain fishin' on a regular basis. Although shallow, it nevertheless harbors plenty of habitat suitable for bass, pickerel, catfish, and the usual pickings of sunfish and perch.

Both of the top-level predators mentioned in the list above grow to impressive proportions here, with reports of individual bass topping the 8-pound mark and pickerel exceeding 4 pounds. The southern half tends to be muddy; anglers typically have higher catch rates in the weeds and stumps of the northern half. Any of a large variety of artificial lures has proved effective, from baitfish-shaped crankbaits to topwater poppers to single-hook spoons (preferably with trailer), and the usual assortment of soft plastics. Live bait, especially large shiners, is equally effective.

Boaters will definitely have the edge here, and the launch facility is located along the western shore not far from East Creek Mill Road (Route 347), a branch off Route 47 in Woodbine. As on the neighboring Lake Nummy (see below), only electric motors are permitted.

Lake Nummy

When the chief of the last local Lenni-Lenape tribe (after whom this water is named) was around, this was little more than a beaver pond on what is now Savage Run, a creek that runs into Roaring Ditch, which in turn dumps into East Creek and finally into Delaware Bay. Years later, it was the Meisle Cranberry Bog, until in the 1930s the Civilian Conservation Corps created the lake found here now for swimming, boating, and fishing.

Although primarily used these days for the former two, Nummy's fishing opportunities merit a visit or two, especially if you happen to find yourself in the area. As in most of the nearby freshwater haunts, chain pickerel and largemouth bass are the two major targets, particularly the former. Although there are no official reports of any smallmouth bass caught or stocked here—and I personally have never seen any—there have been a few vague rumors within the past few years of encounters with these feisty cousins to the largemouth, so it might pay to keep your mind open.

Springtime generally sees good action here, but as the weather warms into May and thereafter, swimmers and boaters start flocking here in greater numbers, and start to fill up the recreational areas on the south and east shores (which include cabins available for overnight camping). Prudence dictates expending your efforts in the other areas of this 26-acre impoundment.

Pickerel go for a number of offerings here; among the more productive are spinnerbaits and shallow-diving crankbaits. Never underestimate the drawing power of a shiner struggling beneath a bobber; jigs entice a number of the bass population as well. Other species here include sunfish and bullheads, both of which are rarely shy about accepting a hook concealed within a doughball or garden worm.

Shorebound anglers and boaters (motors, electric only, are okay) can both score here, as you'll find plenty of overhanging trees, lilies, and other likely habitat reachable by both. The launch area is along Meisle Road, opposite the swimming beach. The lake is more or less in the center of the Belleplain State Forest in Woodbine, reachable from Meisle Road, not far from Belleplain–Woodbine Road (Route 550).

Cumberland County

Clarks Pond

This pond's plural name is a nod to its pluralistic nature. It's located on the Clarks Pond Wildlife Management Area, and actually consists of two, or three, or four separate bodies of water, depending on how you perceive them.

Bass and pickerel rule here. The opportunities for chain pickerel are good pretty much throughout the waters, whereas the bass population is most cooperative in the two waters on either side of Clarks Pond Road. At the easternmost end of the WMA, the water (to which most people are referring when they say "Clarks Pond") goes to between 12 and 15 feet in places; it features good growth, points, and coves that will reward an attentive angler. West of Clarks Pond Road is another fishable area that's much shallower, and then farther west (past the railroad line) is yet another, somewhat deeper water. All of them have fair to good populations of sunfish, yellow perch, bullheads, and carp (the best bets for the latter are in the westernmost section) in addition to the bass and pickerel possibilities.

Shore angling can be good but sometimes cumbersome. Boating is generally better, although boaters will find that getting their craft into the water is most easily accomplished in the easternmost body. The launch area may be reached from a primitive road within the WMA off Clarks Pond Road; exercise due caution, because it hasn't always been clearly marked in the past. Motors—electric only—are allowed in all sections of this WMA's waters.

The WMA is near Fairton and south of Bridgeton, and the primary access roads (Burlington Road and Clarks Pond Road; the latter is also known as Route 722) can be reached most easily from Fairton–Millville Road (Route 698).

Menantico Sand Ponds

For many Garden State anglers, this destination has become a kind of shrine, almost a mecca of bass angling, for one simple reason. It was here, way back in 1980, that the still-standing state-record largemouth bass was caught by Robert Eisele. It was big by any standards, and truly mammoth by northern standards (although this location is actually south of where the Mason-Dixon line would be, were you to extend it east): 10 pounds, 14 ounces.

That was a long time ago, but the fishing remains good to this day. It could be argued that the genetics that produced that lunker of a lifetime still exist in this environment. The system comprises 62 surface acres in an indescribably amorphous shape. There are innumerable drop-offs, underwater islands, laydowns, brushy shores, and the like, so there is plenty of excellent habitat to explore. A corollary to this is the variety of baits that are effective; an abbreviated list includes topwater and shallow plugs and crankbaits, soft plastic worms (both traditional and wacky rigs) and jerkbaits, weedless topwaters, and jigs with trailers. Natural-bait aficionados can use practically any of the commercial baitfish available locally, like shiners, herring, or even killifish.

If largemouth bass aren't your primary target, there is plenty of other action here to occupy you: Chain pickerel, various species of sunfish, a few bullhead varieties, yellow perch, crappie, and the ever-present carp can all add spice to your fishing excursion.

The boat ramp can be accessed via the road off Route 49 (Cumberland Road) in Millville; here, too, motors are allowed as long as they're electric. Shoreline fishing is more difficult (although Eisele caught his historic behemoth from the banks) but doable if you're in good shape. Another excellent option is a float tube if bringing a hard craft is out of the question.

Sunset Lake

If you're in or near Bridgeton, especially with your kids, this should rank as a must on your itinerary. After you've exhausted the fishing opportunities (fat chance, given the 88 acres of varied habitat and a real smorgasbord of excellent freshwater fishing offerings), you can always go to nearby Cohanzick Zoo—reportedly the first one in New Jersey—with plenty of great attractions in its own right.

But this is a book about fishing, so let's start with the bassing opportunities here. The southernmost edge along the main road is an excellent place to begin, as there is a rapid drop-off along that boundary. The water tends to be off-color, meaning lowered visibility, and also that you'll need to use baits that stand out visually or appeal to another of the bass's senses. Live bait is always a good choice; other options can include in-line spinners and spinnerbaits, rattling crankbaits, and topwaters like buzzbaits. This lake also has a wide variety of structure and cover options, so be sure to have a fair selection of styles available to you, including weedless versions. Most largemouths here are 1 to 2 pounds, it's not uncommon to find them from 3 to 5 pounds.

Pickerel anglers can probe the same kinds of locations already mentioned, but don't be too surprised to hook into a tiger muskellunge; the Division of Fish and Wildlife has stocked these aggressive fighters in here. Anglers targeting these fearsome-looking gamefish are well advised to bump up the sizes of their baits, be they real or artificial.

Kids and other panfish specialists of all ages can have a real heyday here, as no fewer than half a dozen varieties (in the sunfish, crappie, perch, and bullhead tribes) are here in good numbers. Crappie anglers especially should find their lust for these scrappy and tasty fish well sated after some time spent here. Carp anglers, always in search of bigger specimens to take their carefully presented baits, should find their needs met as well.

Public access is available from County Road 607 (Beebe Run Road) and West Park Drive in Bridgeton City Park. The boat launch is located along the western shore.

Union Lake

Northern New Jersey has its Lake Hopatcong, and southern New Jersey has this. Much to the dismay, perhaps, of us northerners.

There are essentially no other contenders for the title of Premier Fishery of Southern New Jersey, at least in the freshwater sphere. This almost-900-acre impoundment is part of the Maurice River system, and is one of the central attractions of the Union Lake Wildlife Management Area in Millville. The average depth is about 9 feet, with a maximum going beyond 20 feet centered in the southern section. You'd be hard pressed to find a water with more structure; in addition to the expanses of underwater and emergent growth, lay-downs, drop-offs, points, and coves, a series of Christmas-tree and tire reefs have been planted over the years.

The northern half is characterized by more shallow depths and a greater preponderance of weedy growth, whereas the southern end has greater depths, more riprap along its boundaries (especially close to the dam), and more rocky structure. These characteristics will, of course, dictate much of the fish's behavior, depending on species, times of day, and season.

Largemouth bass opportunities here are manifold, and both size and numbers are good—it isn't unusual to catch your daily limit here, and specimens topping 6 pounds are seen on a regular basis. The tools that will work best depend on the specific area targeted as well as time of day, but speaking very generally some of the most popular choices include dark-colored plastic worms (rigged Texas style, Carolina style, or wacky), crankbaits, plugs, and jigs/trailers. Don't be afraid to experiment.

How about smallmouths? The Division of Fish and Wildlife has been experimenting with smallmouth bass here since the beginning of the new millennium, and the fishery may be catching on—although it's still unclear whether the species can perpetuate itself. But the habitat is certainly more than adequate for good growth and holdover, particular in the southern half of the lake. Specimens are caught while working jigs along rocky substrates, trolling swimming lures, and with smaller spinnerbaits.

Chain pickerel love the weedy areas, especially in the northern half, and share that habitat with some good-sized largemouths. Pickerel will take some of the same baits that will entice largemouths but seem to prefer the real thing . . . except during late day and early evening, when they'll often whack anything that's moving. Tiger muskies have been introduced to these waters as well, and sometimes turn up unexpectedly when anglers are targeting their smaller cousins, or indeed many of the other species.

Don't overlook the striped bass population—and I don't just mean the hybrid varieties. Full-strain stripers do exist here, as shown by recent electrofishing surveys, and some are sizable indeed. Some think that the pure strains have resulted from anglers practicing catch-and-release for them elsewhere in the Maurice River, but however they got here, they get hungry just as often as any other fish does.

If you prefer other varieties of big fish, channel catfish and carp are both doing very well, and in fact this location is one of the few in New Jersey where channel catfish are actively reproducing, according to sources at the Division of Fish and Wildlife. In springtime, look for the carp cruising some of the shallows; as usual, these large fellows are best coaxed with doughballs, corn, fruit-sweetened bait, or various combinations.

Panfish make up an essential part of the fishery here, both as midlevel participants in the food hierarchy and as targetable gamefish. The predominant species caught are a variety of sunfish including bluegills, yellow and white perch, black crappie, and eels.

The facilities are very good for both boaters and non-boaters. Two boat launches service the lake. One is run by the town of Millville and is accessed by taking Sharp Street from Route 49 and looking for the launch area on the left. The other is owned and operated by the division; it's located on the western shore, accessible from Carmel Road. The latter has a parking area for 50 vehicles with trailers and is lit for nighttime fishing. Outboard motors are allowed at Union as long as they have less than 10 horsepower.

Willow Grove Lake

This 120-acre body of water along the Cumberland–Salem border gets water from Still Run and Scotland Run from the north, and its effluent forms the beginning of the Maurice River. It has one large island near the southern end and a couple of smaller ones farther north. The average depth is a mere 3 to 3.5 feet, and it doesn't get much deeper than about 6 feet—and then only in a few places.

Think South Jersey, think shallow and weedy, think stained and cedar . . . yes, here's another good pickerel spot. But the largemouth bass here aren't too shabby, either; many anglers have named this spot as the place they caught their largest New Jersey bass, as it isn't too unusual to see some individuals topping the 5- and 6-pound mark. Spinnerbaits are a good starting choice; try slow-rolling them through some of the shallower spots toward the deeper ones in the center. There are plenty of pads and stumps, so try bumping your spinnerbait against the latter or pulling some weedless combinations through the former. Topwaters will also get the attention of both gamefish varieties, especially during low-light periods.

This fishing core is supplemented by the usual assortment of panfish—bluegills, yellow perch, bullheads, and crappie—and the carp population is often willing to play tug-of-war as well. Located in the northernmost tip of the county, it can be accessed from Route 690 in the northern section of Vineland. There is little in the way of launch facilities, but the lake is perfectly suited for a small canoe or johnboat fitted with an electric motor.

Gloucester County

Alcyon Lake

To come here is to immerse yourself into the past. This lake is one of the central features of Alcyon Lake Park, the land for which was purchased by the Carr brothers in 1888. It opened in 1892 (named Alcyon by one of the brothers, Henry, because he felt that *halcyon* was too difficult to pronounce) as a general amusement park, with the lake available for fishing and boating. The lake and park later suffered from neglect, abuse, and pollution, and by the late 20th century became the nation's first Superfund site. The area has since been cleaned and reclaimed, although sedimentation continues to plague the lake.

Nevertheless, good angling persists. The best is for chain pickerel, crappie, and sunfish, but largemouth bass account for a good percentage of the anglers who come here, and more than one carp angler has departed this place with a big smile.

A pier allows for increased ease of launching a small boat, and electric motors are allowed. The park and lake are in the northeast part of Pitman, bordered by Holly Avenue, Cedar Avenue, and Carr Avenue.

Harrisonville Lake

Located within the Harrisonville Lake Wildlife Management Area, this 30-acre spot straddling the Gloucester–Salem border may not seem like much when you first see it, but the angling potential definitely merits it a place on your "to-fish" list. First of all, the state stocks it in springtime with hatchery trout, providing some immediate opportunities for anglers both experienced and novice. Mealworms and small spinners—especially roostertails—are favorites at this time of year, and others also do well with garden worms and corn kernels.

The annual trout stocking here has had other effects as well. The resident largemouths and chain pickerels have been feasting on this free food for many seasons, resulting in very healthy populations of both species, which have learned to home in on trouty-looking food sources. As the trout season (and stocking) reaches full force by the end of April, a wise angler will start using trout-colored crankbaits near the lake's access area (where the stocking trucks dump their loads) in order to tap into this phenomenon. Anglers have reported days here of upward of a dozen bass, all in the 2- to 4-pound range.

As the weather warms, these predators start looking for alternate forage after the gratuitous trout have stopped appearing, and will start to react to more classic baits like plastic worms, topwater baits, jigs, and spinnerbaits. By the time summer hits full flower, the surface of the water is often choked with surface growth, mandating the use of frogs, rats, and other baits designed to skitter over such top foliage. Other species include sunfish, crappie, perch, bullheads, channel catfish, and carp.

Some shoreline access through the WMA is available, but much of the perimeter is privately owned. Boaters can bring car-top boats and use electric motors if so desired, although the lake's somewhat diminutive size makes rowing or paddling a perfectly adequate means of getting about. It's located just south of Harrisonville; the access road is named Lake Street in Gloucester County and Harrisonville Lake Road in Salem County.

Iona Lake

It might seem that this water is little more than an exaggerated version of the swamplands that surround it, but plenty of anglers have found out otherwise. Most of the lake's 32 acres is a mere couple of feet deep, and the northernmost end sometimes struggles to cover the weeds. It does get a tad deeper—to 3 and 4 feet—in the southern half. And during much of the open-water season, the grassy weed growth is a sight to behold.

Once you get past all this, however, you'll find yourself in a position to catch fish. As in Harrisonville Lake, described above, the yearly infusion of stocked trout provides both an early-season angling opportunity as well as important forage, and the bass and pickerel populations take advantage of this. After finishing with the usual round of trout angling in April and May, salmonidlike crankbaits in these months and even into early June can produce. By the time the summer solstice hits, however, chances are that trout will be but a distant memory (if indeed bass and pickerel have such things)—and there will undoubtedly be too much weed growth to work these baits effectively anymore. Now is the time for weedless worms and other soft plastics, and a skillfully wielded single-hook spoon can turn fish heads as well.

Although southern New Jersey has a reputation for some fine pickerel angling (and justifiably so), don't overlook the excellent largemouth opportunities that are abundant in the area.

The standard panfish assortment can also serve to help keep the younger set occupied or provide an alternate source of amusement for the veteran; these include bluegills, crappie, yellow perch, and bullheads. The lake may be found near Porchtown, along Route 612 (Taylor Road). Boating is allowed but motors aren't, and the launch area is directly accessible from Route 612.

Malaga Lake

Sometimes it seems like Malaga Lake is schizophrenic: On some days it can be truly memorable, while on others you're left scratching your head and wondering where all the fish went. But if you can get here on an "on" day, or apply assiduous analysis to your techniques on the other days, you'll find your time here well spent. Just ask any of the South Jersey bass clubs that list Malaga as a permanent stop on their tournament schedule.

The 105-acre impoundment on the Still Run has a relatively uniform depth as you traverse its length in a north–south direction. The periphery drops down more sharply along the eastern shore than the western; the maximum depth (about 9 feet) is attained in a small area close to the dam. Discolored water, typical of this region, prevails, and there are plenty of biological structure components: stumps and both underwater and emergent growth. Pickerel are nearly ubiquitous in waters like this, and the largemouth population does well here also.

Bait considerations are fairly standard: shallow-running plugs and jerkbaits, alternating with buzzbaits and poppers, for topwater action; spinnerbaits and jigs for deeper probing. Live shiners or herring are always a good bet, while smaller natural offerings like garden worms will entice some of the panfish here, as well as the occasional carp.

Some shoreline angling is possible here; waders can be useful if you have them. Boaters can get going by using the ramp on the lake's east side (Malaga Lake Park along Malaga Park Drive), but use extra caution if the water is low. Access can also be gained on the western shore via Malaga Lake Boulevard, where shoreline fishing, boat launching, and parking are possible on any nonprivate ground. Electric motors are permitted. Malaga Park Drive and Malaga Lake Boulevard can both be reached from Route 40 north of Vineland.

Wilson Lake

Named after the family that constructed the dam in 1840 for sawmill power, this impoundment on Scotland Run is one of the central features of 940-acre Scotland Run Park.

Prevailing water quality favors the native pickerel and perch populations in this 58-acre lake, both of which are rated highly by the state as well as by visiting anglers. But the largemouth population is not to be sneezed at, either; in recent years, although an angler may not always catch a legal limit here, there have been some genuinely jaw-dropping braggers caught. I'm talking fish in the 6- to 8-pound range, enough to turn the head of the most jaded bass hunter.

Depths drop off most quickly along the long eastern shore, making this good place to start. Other areas to spend extra time include the weed beds in and near the deepest parts of the lake, corresponding mostly to the creek's channel running along the water's length. The coves and points are always worth some extra casts as well. Like most of the area's waters of this type, Wilson Lake shows substantial weed growth early in the season and becomes overgrown or close to it quickly. By late spring weedless, or at least weed-resistant, baits become more and more critical to efficient angling.

Sunfish, bullheads, carp, and crappie complete the offerings available here. Classic live-bait offerings are best for these, and some people have found that small spinners take their share of panfish, with the occasional pickerel or bass grabbing one to provide a nice surprise.

Boating and motoring (electric only) are helpful here, and the park has a ramp in good condition. Scotland Run Park is located in the Fries Mills section of Clayton, just north of Clayton–Williamsburg Road and east of Fries Mill Road.

Ocean County

Lake Carasaljo and Lake Manetta

If you're a new visitor to Carasaljo Park of Lakewood, you might have trouble pronouncing its name—until you remember that it was named after three daughters of wealthy landowner and industrialist Joseph W. Brick: Carol, Sally, and Josephine. Some veteran anglers have opined that this 70-acre lake's heyday has come and gone, but you'll have a tough time convincing the younger guys who are reeling fish in that that has any truth to it.

Pickerel, pickerel, and more pickerel. Their location is dictated in some measure by the presence and density of weeds and some standing timber, but fish can be caught virtually all over the lake. A number of artificial baits will bring them to hand—try some topwaters like buzzbaits and

Jitterbugs around daybreak and again at dusk, with plastic worms and spinnerbaits good choices during the day. If you target these pickerel, chances are good you'll come up with an occasional largemouth bass or two, possibly of good size. If you target the bass, however, it may well be that all you'll see are pickerel (at least that's what seems to happen to me).

The other fish that many people target are crappie, followed by sunfish and perch. Carp and channel catfish are also here, although the latter have been stocked fairly recently by the Division of Fish and Wildlife and that fishery has yet to come to full fruition.

Most of the angling here is restricted to shoreline only, but on the flip side virtually the entire lake's periphery is open, making for a leisurely half- or full-day walkaround as you fish. Those who want to increase their mobility, however, can take advantage of a local boat rental program available during part of the year. Be aware of the swimming area, of course, although that has been subject to occasional closure in recent years due to high microbial content in the water.

Carasaljo Lake is in the northern part of Lakewood, near Georgian Court College and bordered by North and South Lake Drives, North Hope Chapel Road, and Route 9.

Lake Manetta, just south, is connected by a short creek to Carasaljo. Although access to the smaller 18-acre pond isn't quite as simple here, it's worth giving it a go if you get tired of Carasaljo or the park starts filling up with too many people for your liking. The fishing opportunities are nearly identical, and it's pretty much shoreline fishing or nothing. Go to the southeastern tip of Carasaljo and head due south, crossing South Lake Drive, Central Avenue, and Caranetta Drive. And there you are.

Colliers Mills and Turn Mill Ponds

These are two of the four primary fishable bodies of water within the Colliers Mills Wildlife Management Area in the northern part of the county, in Jackson and Plumsted

Townships. They merit more discussion than the others (Kennedy Pond and Success Lake) due to better fisheries and easier access. The two are very similar in a number of ways. Both are fairly shallow and weedy, and the fishing is dominated by chain pickerel, yellow perch, and sunfish. Some largemouth bass are here, and in fact the larger of the two (Turn Mill Pond, at about 100 acres) is the occasional site of a local bass tournament. Both have also been subject to stocking of channel catfish; the results have been modest at best, but a determined catfish specialist is likely to have moderate success.

Boating, with electric motors, is allowed in both waters, but only Turn Mill has a boat ramp. Shoreline angling is easy for both, around most of their peripheries. Both are located on the western edge of the WMA, and are accessible via Route 640 (also known locally either as Hawkin Road or Prospertown–Colliers Mills Road). Turn east onto East Colliers Mills Road to get to either pond; Colliers Mills is the one to your left (north), while Turn Mill is south.

Prospertown Lake

This 80-acre lake is something of a conundrum, as are so many of New Jersey's lakes. It offers an outdoor experience that many consider to be close to "natural" (whatever that means), yet it abuts one of the busiest and noisiest attractions in the state—Six Flags Amusement Park. In fact, from much of Prospertown Lake you can easily see the roller-coaster ride, and it isn't unusual to hear the noises from the park.

And the truth of the matter is that it provides some of the best bass and pickerel angling in the region, yet remains relatively underutilized. Perhaps the proximity to Six Flags keeps some people away; perhaps it's the "no motors" regulation in force here. But for those willing to get past these minor encumbrances, it's a great place to do some fishin'.

It is also one of only two still-water locations in Ocean County that receives a yearly infusion of trout each spring.

The allocation tends to be on the small side, and the predominant species is brook trout (undoubtedly due to that species' hardiness, at least relative to its kin the brown and rainbow trout), but this nevertheless provides some early-season action for area fishermen . . . and some nutritional bonus for the high-end underwater predators.

Make no mistake: The potential is here for some bragging-sized fish in both the micropterid and esocid families. Over the past few years, there have been reports of bass in the 3- to 5-pound range, and one claimant alleges to have caught and released a largemouth behemoth that weighed 9.5 pounds. Pickerel up to 4 pounds are not too unusual a tale told here. Perch and sunfish are also numerous, as are bullheads. The occasional channel catfish comes in as well, making this a satisfying venue for almost any freshwater practitioner.

The average depth is about 4 feet, and maxes out at around 10, particularly near the dam by the parking area. The lake is perfectly suited for small car-top boats—and also popular with kayakers. It's best to work the banks and coves carefully with surface lures during low-light periods, and jigs, spinnerbaits, and crankbaits at other times. Soft plastic baits will generally produce as well. Not a few ice fishermen have caught their share of pickerel, perch, and even largemouths during the coldest months, so if there is safe ice by all means give it a try.

Look for the access road in the northwest tip of Ocean County on Route 537 (Monmouth Road), just south of Six Flags in Prospertown.

Lake Shenandoah

In June 2004, as a result of runoff due to nearby fires, thousands of this popular and scenic lake's gamefish came floating to the surface. But time and cleanup efforts have rectified that situation nicely, as evidenced by continued angler success.

The lake is the central feature of Lake Shenandoah County Park, and comprises about 50 acres. The mean depth is approximately 10 feet; the deepest areas reach about 20 feet. Good but not excessive weed growth characterizes the water here, making it suitable for a wide range of fish. In fact, it is the other of the two Ocean County lakes (see Prospertown Lake, above) that receives trout each spring—a combination of brook, brown, and rainbow trout. Most that are caught by April and May anglers respond to garden or mealworms, killies, and small spinners.

It is, however, the largemouth bass and chain pickerel that attract most rod-wielding sojourners. The varied habitat and extensive forage base—and lack of night fishing, since it's a county property—allow these two gamefish to reach impressive proportions. Tales have been told of 8- and 9-pound largemouths, and of pickerel exceeding 2 feet in length. Many who target these larger individuals prefer to use baitfish, especially shiners. Others who don't want to bother keeping a collection of fish alive and healthy while they fish instead opt for a variety of artificial lures, including surface models outside the hottest days of summer, and soft plastic variants in July and August. In addition to targeting the weeded areas, the sharp drop-offs along the southern shore hold some promise, as do the floating and attached docks. And it may not be necessary to stray too far from the fishing piers, located near the park's entry point and on the eastern shore.

The other fish that some concentrate on, albeit with a lower success rate overall, is the tiger muskellunge, which has been stocked here by the Division of Fish and Wildlife for years now. As always when targeting these dentally unchallenged creatures, it is essential to use a wire leader to avoid break-offs. And panfish are here in abundance as well, including a couple of sunfish species, yellow perch, and bullheads. The carp population here is not overwhelming but can provide a nice surprise or two to those using small baits to target fish on the bottom.

Even if you don't have a boat of your own, you can rent one here from the on-site facility, and top off your angling equipment needs from the bait and tackle concession. Shoreline anglers have plenty of places to toss in their line as well, including the aforementioned fishing docks.

The park is in Lakewood, just west of Exit 90 off the Garden State Parkway, reachable from Route 88 (Ocean Avenue) and across the street from the Ocean County Park.

Salem County

Elmer Lake

People have been wanting to get better public launch facilities at this 45-acre lake located on the eastern border of the town of Elmer. The reason is simple: They want to get to some of the noteworthy bass angling here. Besides hosting a good population of largemouths, the fishery is typical of the region, with pickerel, perch, and crappie coming in as close seconds after the largemouths. Sunfish and carp numbers are high as well, making it a popular angling spot.

Good depth distributions help to keep these populations' health in good order. The average depth is somewhere around 5 feet, and places go down to 8 and 10 feet. There are plenty of weeds and stumps to provide cover for the scaled residents; these should probably be your first stops when exploring here. Early- and late-season anglers do well with faster-moving lures like rattling crankbaits and spinnerbaits, and summertime folks are successful with rat and frog imitations dragged over the surface growth.

There is a cleared area at the north end of the lake (Route 40) from which you can launch a small car-top craft; otherwise the shoreline angling is limited. Although there are plans to install a ramp in this area, these have been stalled due to the expense and effort involved. Anybody needing a ramp can try the private one behind the lawn mower repair operation located on Main Street (Route 648).

Laurel Lake

Located on the eastern outskirts of Quinton, this is a 17-acre lake whose perimeter is mostly privately held. Still, there's enough public access that any angler in the area would do well to give it a try. It's mostly a sunfish-and-bass pond; these two species interact closely in the ongoing biological drama of the environment. Pickerel are present as well, although fewer in number than the largemouths, and a good smattering of panfish species live here also: bluegills, sunfish, perch, crappie, and bullheads. The channel catfish here have not responded well to the environment, and the jury is still out as to their long-term survival. Finally, the carp contingent is steady; some double-digit specimens are caught here each season.

The pond is north of Route 48, and is bordered by Lake Avenue and Waterworks Road. Car-top vessels are allowed, as are electric motors.

Maskells Mill Pond

Part of the Maskells Mill Pond Wildlife Area, which recently expanded with the acquisition of an old clay mine property, this L-shaped pond is an unassuming waterway that is perfect for some informal, no-frills angling. Shoreline access is somewhat limited and there is little in the way of any kind of launching facilities, but a lone angler with a canoe, or a pair of fishermen with a small rowboat, can do just fine here. Electric motors are fine for such excursions, but a pair of oars (or a paddle if you're canoeing) is really all you need.

There are a fair variety of depths; the average is about 4 feet and the deepest goes to 8 feet near the Route 658 access area. The northern branch has more in the way of explorable coves and fishable points, while the east spur has more fish-holding drop-offs near its center. Both are worth casting to: try topwaters and unweighted soft plastics in the former, and slow-rolled spinnerbaits, jigs, and weighted worms (Texas rigging is good) in the latter. Both of these approaches should work on the largemouth bass and chain pickerel population.

(In years past it was predominantly a pickerel pond, but the bass have been doing substantially better within the past decade.)

Panfish, for sure. Good and eager populations of bluegills, sunfish, perch, and crappie will take any of the standard offerings (garden worms, mealworms, small spinners); try small leadhead jigs tipped with small plastic grubs for the crappie. Those who prefer to sit and wait can throw their bottom-hugging baits in to tempt the bullheads, eels, or carp.

The pond is a few miles northeast of the Mad Horse Creek Wildlife Management Area and south of Quinton; the three main access points are along Route 658 (Maskells Mill Road), Mill Pond Road, and Batter Cake Road.

Parvin Lake

This 0.7-mile-long lake is one of the featured attractions of Parvin State Park in the southern tip of the county. The total surface acreage is 95, with a mean depth of about 4 feet. It does go down to about 6 feet in a couple of places, most notably in front of the dam that controls the flow into Muddy Run and near the swimming area.

This picture could have been taken anywhere in New Jersey. Sunfish are definitely a staple of the freshwater angler's repertoire.

Another popular place among largemouth anglers, "slow but steady" might be one way to describe this place. The numbers are there but aren't overwhelming; on the other hand, a few hours of focused fishing is likely to reward your efforts with at least a couple of fish. And, as a bonus, there are days when they are more willing, and there is always a chance for a memorable fish, considering the reports of specimens up to about 7 pounds. (Note that Parvin Lake is one of the state's Lunker Lake members; the daily limit is three, and each one must be at least 15 inches.) The areas opposite the bathing beach and in the back half—farthest from the dam, with depths of about 2 to 4 feet—can be worth some extra effort.

Shoreline structure can yield some fish, including pickerel and crappie, on topwater lures like poppers; smaller offerings can bring in perch or sunfish. There are also excellent carp and bullhead populations here, making this a well-rounded fishery.

There is a boat ramp available, and electric motors are permitted. The ramp and parking area are located just south of the intersection of Parvin Mill Road (Route 645) and Almond Road (Route 540) in Centerton, not far from the Salem–Cumberland border.

Rainbow Lake

Rainbow Lake offers mixed bag of advantages and disadvantages for the visiting angler, but once you're on this 77-acre water the chances are that you'll have a better-than-average day—especially if largemouth bass are your quarry. If you're shoreline angling or launching a small car-top boat, you should have no problems, but if you're using a trailered boat then caution is warranted at the boat ramp. (Electric motors are permitted.) Watch out for your tow vehicle and the ruts at the ramp, and keep an eye on the water level, which fluctuates a lot.

The other thing to keep aware of is that there have been conflicts between anglers and some of the private residents surrounding the lake. Suffice it to say that it behooves you to observe all applicable regulations, as well as rules of conduct for good and polite behavior, even when you can't see anybody watching you (because they might be anyway).

Once you're here and fishing, try working the southwesternmost cove and across the lake in the northern tip to start. Slowly presented plastics seem to be key here; try worms rigged traditionally or wacky, and other imitation forms like crayfish. Some good bass are here, including those in the 7- and 8-pound range. You're likely to hook other species as well, including chain pickerel, yellow perch, and crappie, while engaged in this activity. Sunfish, carp, and bullhead are also here for those who prefer them or want to get their kids started in fishing.

Now a part of a Wildlife Management Area, the facility includes parking, portable comfort facilities, and the ramp. It's located on Landis Avenue (Route 56) between Alvine Road (Route 655) and Big Oak Road (Route 658) west of Norma, near Parvin State Park and Union Lake Wildlife Management Area.

11

SOUTHERN NEW JERSEY RIVERS AND STREAMS

Mullica River

Known primarily among anglers in general as a great saltwater angling fishery (including the famous spot where the river's waters meet the Great Bay at Graveling Point and produce great early-season striped bass opportunities), farther upstream into the Pinelands the Mullica River has some very worthwhile freshwater opportunities as well. For many anglers these center on chain pickerel fishing, but other species that many folks happily target include largemouth bass, perch, and crappie. Catfish and eels are encountered occasionally also.

One of the best-known starting points for your Mullica quest is Batsto Village, located within the Wharton State Forest in the southern part of Burlington County. Fishing from the banks is fine, but those with more mobility will do better launching their boat from the ramp operated there (there is a small fee for each use, or you can purchase a yearly launch permit). Electric motors only are allowed.

Look for your quarry in all the old familiar places—lay-downs, weedy areas, and the like—of which there are plenty. Live bait shines, but anybody preferring to use artificials can do well with shallow-diving crankbaits and spinnerbaits. Work areas both up- and downstream of Batsto, and don't be shy about trying some of the feeder tributaries.

Batsto Village is located on Route 542, 8 miles east of Hammonton.

Rancocas Creek

One of the more popular tributary feeders to the Delaware
River, a number of this flow's branches originate in the
eastern and southern portions of Burlington County and con-
verge into the North and South Branches. These streams
meet at the edge of Rancocas State Park, and the main
Rancocas then joins the Delaware at Delran.

A good assortment of fish species awaits the Rancocas
angler, depending on the location and time of year. During
spring, many anglers target the striped bass in the main stem
and western parts of the North and South Branches as they
move through their area in their annual spawning behavior.
Popular baits include worms (nightcrawlers are good, and
some anglers like bloodworms) or herring on high/low rigs;
others like a variety of baitfish-imitating lures. The main
stem, particularly close to the Delaware, is also known as a
good spot for sizable carp, targeted in late April into June.

Largemouth bass are another important gamefish here,
and in fact some anglers quit the Delaware specifically to
search the Rancocas for this popular fish. Anybody targeting
largemouths must bear in mind that tidal current patterns
have a significant impact on bass behavior and location. They
affect other fish species, too, of course, but tidal patterns seem
to have an exaggerated effect on bass. During slack-tide
periods, the flow may seem calm, even sluggish, but at high or
low tide the current can be deceptively fast.

Channel catfish are also caught from these waters, and it
isn't unusual to see individuals in the 5-pound range or larger.
Preferred baits include nightcrawler gobs, chicken livers, cut
baitfish, and specialized commercial catfish products. In the
quieter backwater and eddy sections, it's also common to
catch white perch, crappie, and sunfish.

Access is available at a number of locations. Right at the
mouth of the river, Amico Island Park in Delran, accessible
from Norman Avenue, is a good choice. As you head farther
east, places to try include Mill Creek Park in Willingboro

(Route 626), Rancocas State Park just east of the New Jersey Turnpike, and some of the Mount Holly Parks (Creek Island Park, Monroe Street Park, Ironworks Park, Smithville County Park).

Maurice River and Menantico Creek

Located entirely within (or along, if you prefer) Cumberland County, the Maurice begins its life under this name as the effluent from Willow Grove Lake. It courses downstream for some miles, defining the border with Salem County, until it reaches Union Lake in Millville. From the downstream end of this water, it then proceeds essentially uninterrupted until it dumps into the Delaware Bay. There is some heightened salinity in this stretch, which of course increases until its terminus. Menantico Creek, originating at the Menantico Sand Ponds, flows into the river at the southern end of Millville and represents the approximate location at which the salinity level becomes too high for freshwater fish.

This system is easily one of the more popular for freshwater anglers in South Jersey, and with good reason. In springtime, anglers are targeting striped and largemouth bass; many go for the herring that are moving through here, especially in the parts south of Union Lake. There is some sporadic bass and pickerel fishing along the northern parts of the river, as well as some springtime trout stocking in Vineland and other locations, but these pale compared with the activity found south of the Union Lake Dam.

During March and April, plenty of people line up to fish along the shores and on the bridges spanning the main river to get their share of the herring that swim here each year. Typical specimens are about 6 to perhaps 15 inches, and many are caught with shiny metallic lures wielded in an up-and-down jigging motion. Those who aren't targeting these cute little swimmers are likely seeking the creatures chasing the cute little swimmers—namely, the striped bass. Herring specialists do well standing on the Route 49 bridge (staying well aware of the vehicular traffic going back and forth, of course) and the dam on Sharp Street.

Those with striped bass on the brain tend to do better with appropriately heavier tackle. The two most popular natural baits here are probably bloodworms and (surprise, surprise) herring. Some spend time filling their herring buckets, then switch over to their striper outfits with a fresh supply of fresh, match-the-hatch-exactly bait.

Those who prefer to go for largemouth bass can find their quarry here as well, but different people seem to have different experiences—some do consistently well for both size and numbers, while others consider this stretch of river to be only so-so at best for the black bass. Either way, however, bigmouths are undeniably available here, and it is by no means unusual to arrive at the Maurice only to encounter some bass tournament or another in progress.

Prevailing wisdom holds that the best angling opportunities for all of the freshwater-only species (meaning, those besides stripers) are concentrated in the stretch between Route 49 and the Union Lake Dam. This tends to result in a sizable population of fisherfolk on weekends in spring and summer, so if you have the opportunity to visit this river on a weekday, you'll undoubtedly find the crowds less overwhelming. Other species include pickerel, catfish, and some panfish.

Probably the most important tributary to the Maurice is the Menantico Creek, where many find largemouth angling to be well within the bounds of satisfaction. And because of the water's tidal behavior, the resident fish often seem immune to the lethargy that often hits largemouths during the hottest summer days; the action continues unabated during these scorching months. In addition to the standard fare of structure and cover to explore, be sure to try the pilings supporting the bridges holding Routes 47 and 55 over the water, at the southern end of Millville. Be wary of high tides, however; many times it's difficult if not downright dangerous to boat underneath these overpasses when the water level is up. And unless you're very familiar with the upstream portions of the creek closer to the Menantico Sands Ponds, it's wiser to limit your excursion upstream to that second bridge (Route 55).

Boaters will find a good public launch facility at the end of Fowser Road, on the east bank of the river off Route 47; all the areas discussed here are easily available from this launch point. Those without a boat can fish off the Route 49 (Main Street) bridge near the intersection of Route 47, although it will be necessary to park elsewhere and walk over. Dam fishermen can access Sharp Street from the south via Route 49, and from the north by turning off Route 47.

Metedeconk River

The most interesting freshwater portions of this river are located primarily within Ocean County, and are made up of the North and South Branches. These coalesce into the main stem in between the Garden State Parkway and Forge Pond in Bricktown; the river continues from the pond to Barnegat Bay. Early-spring anglers get their share of angling opportunities from the liberal sprinkling of hatchery trout that are dumped into the river by the Division of Fish and Wildlife, which accounts for much of the angling pressure that the river receives.

Many of the stocking points occur at overpassing bridges, and these tend to attract the highest numbers of anglers also. If you don't mind competing with these comrades on stocking days, fine. If you prefer to avoid them, however, it's really just a simple matter to walk up- or downstream 100 yards or more, seeking the next likely-looking pool or eddy. The standard baits will do you justice: garden worms, mealworms, fathead minnows, and small gold- or silver-colored spinners. Fly anglers can find a few spots where casting is reasonably unencumbered, and can use any of a number of surface or subsurface flies. Some of my favorites for hatchery trout are egg patterns, Glo Worms, and San Juan Worms.

Don't think that once the state stops dumping these salmonids in here come the end of May, the river fishing is done. There are plenty of pickerel, catfish, and panfish that need to keep feeding during summer and autumn months, and many of the same places where you concentrated your trout fishing will hold year-round residents. One good stretch that should serve for most, if not all, of the species discussed here is on the North Branch from Lanes Mill Road down to the confluence with the South Branch. Some of the roads passing over the North Branch where access is simplest are County Line Road, Ridge Avenue, Brook Road, and Squankum Road (these are all in Lakewood). Along the South Branch, try the park area parallel to Route 88 (Ocean Avenue).

Toms River

Northern New Jersey generally gets more press for stream trout fishing, with its Musconetcong, Pequest, and Raritan Rivers, but the south has the Toms River. Undoubtedly the primary trout stream in the warmer sections of our state, the Toms provides one of the few trout-holding waters where stocked specimens can survive, and even thrive, throughout the year, providing some real chances for lunker catches.

One section of the river in particular is the focus of most anglers, and is part of the state's Year-Round Trout Conservation Area. This has its ups and downs—in the former category, it means that you'll undoubtedly find some fine trouting here, and it also means that you can alleviate your March cabin fever by fishing here during the pre-stocking period in late March and early April, when the majority of trout-stocked waters are closed to fishing altogether (as long as you practice strict catch-and-release angling). On the downside, it means that you're liable to be seeing more anglers working the same waters than perhaps you might like, and only artificial baits (flies, spinners, and the like) are allowed. Too, during the regular season, only one trout may be kept, and it must be at least 15 inches in length (except for in-season trout-stocking days, when no creel is allowed).

The conservation area begins at the southern boundary of Riverwood Park in Dover, and extends about a mile beyond to the Route 571 crossing. Both ends are readily reached, the former by parking in or near the park, and the latter from Route 571 directly (although parking nearby may prove somewhat of a challenge). If you choose the northern approach, it has the advantage of providing ready angling opportunities within the park itself where the conservation area rules do not apply, and the trout

The Toms River is undoubtedly the premier trout stream in southern New Jersey, and an angler can satisfy his or her yen for rainbow, brook, or brown trout (pictured here) accordingly.

opportunities there are worthwhile in their own right. Too, if you wish to try angling from a canoe, feel free to bring one; you can launch it from within the park.

Throughout these areas, those with proper wading gear will have a distinct advantage due to the often thick foliage lining the banks (which is also part of the reason the aquatic habitat here is so favorable for trout); just be sure to exercise all due caution when negotiating this growth, as poison ivy is common. If you'd like to try your luck farther downstream beyond the conservation area, you won't be wasting your time—but keep in mind that you'll need that freshwater fishing license (and trout stamp, if you're targeting trout) as long as you're upstream of the Garden State Parkway bridge.

Don't think that this is the only place in the Toms where trout are willing to grab your disguised hook. A number of locations upstream also receive their share of raceway graduates. One such spot is in Jackson. The area of the tree farm, part of the State Forestry Station between Veterans Highway and Bowman Road, is also popular with area trout anglers. Here, anything goes in the bait department, whether natural or artificial, and those using mealworms and garden worms generally see good numbers of brook and brown trout.

Finally, the favorable habitat helps more than just the trout. Other species like pickerel, eels, and assorted panfish have their dietary needs met here as well, and can provide an amusing diversion from your trout quest.

AFTERWORD

BEFORE WE PART company, there are a few points worth bringing up. The first has to do with the protection of our resource. This becomes increasingly important in our state as more and more people compete for the finite land and water within our boundaries.

Catch-and-release is something you've undoubtedly heard of, and I encourage you to practice it diligently. This needn't be done at the expense of the occasional meal of fresh fish, however. There is absolutely nothing wrong with bringing home a limit of freshwater bass once or twice a season, or having a nice perch fry on a cold winter's day, or baking that one lake trout this spring. But the measure of what constitutes "excessive" must be made far more carefully these days than ever before.

If you're fishing with your five-year-old son, don't toss every one of those bluegills into a bucket. Keep just a few of the larger ones, and make the proper release of the smaller guys part of your child's whole fishing experience. If you've decided that you're going to bring home a meal of walleye for yourself that evening, do you really need a full day's limit of three to have a satisfying meal (especially considering that each one must be at least 18 inches long)? As the old saying goes, "Limit your catch; don't catch your limit." At least not on any kind of a regular basis.

Since we're speaking of the possibilities in bringing home a dinner of fresh fish, this brings up another point. Our environment has been subject to poisoning and contamination from industrial processes for so many decades now that it's a given that there are contaminants out there. Unfortunately, these toxins have been a part of our ecosystem for so long that they've become well entrenched within the food chain, including the freshwater fish that we love to seek. This means that, first of all, you now have another reason to limit the numbers of fish you bring home to consume. It also means that if you still intend to have these meals, it would behoove you to find out the recommended maximum amounts of fish that you should consume within a given month or year. This information is available from the Division of Fish and Wildlife, the state Department of Environmental Protection, and your local health authorities.

I urge anybody who is concerned with either or both of these issues to become more active. The easiest way to do so is to join a local chapter of any of the conservation-minded organizations: Trout Unlimited, the New Jersey BASS Federation, Muskies, Inc., the New Jersey State Federation of Sportsmen's Clubs, and plenty more.

• • •

There are some great resources where one can find more information on the fishing opportunities within the state of New Jersey. These include:

• *New Jersey Fish and Wildlife Digest*, January issue, covering freshwater fishing, published annually by the Division of Fish and Wildlife.

• *New Jersey Places to Fish*, a short brochure summarizing many of the public locations in the state, available free at Division of Fish and Wildlife facilities.

• *New Jersey Lake Survey Fishing Maps Guide* and *New Jersey's Fishing Streams and the Delaware River*, both published by

New Jersey Sportsmen's Guides (Somerdale, New Jersey). The first is a compendium of lake maps, showing depth contours and more, plus some quick fishing tips, for many of our state's lakes; the second is a series of articles on fishing some of New Jersey's streams and rivers.

• Finally, the personnel at the Division of Fish and Wildlife are often available for information; they may be reached by telephone at 609-292-2965, or online at www. state.nj.us/dep/fgw/index.htm.

INDEX